P9-CBG-437

MODERN WORLD NATIONS

Iran
Second Edition

Masoud Kheirabadi *, 1951⌐*
Portland State University

Series Editor
Charles F. Gritzner
South Dakota State University

CHELSEA HOUSE
An Infobase Learning Company

Frontispiece: Flag of Iran

Cover: The northern district of Tehran, Iran.

Iran

Copyright © 2011 by Infobase Learning

Chelsea House
An imprint of Infobase Learning
132 West 31st Street
New York, NY 10001

Library of Congress Cataloging-in-Publication Data
Kheirabadi, Masoud, 1951-
  Iran / by Masoud Kheirabadi. — 2nd ed.
    p. cm. — (Modern world nations)
  Includes bibliographical references and index.
  ISBN 978-1-60413-939-6 (hardcover)
  1. Iran—Juvenile literature. I. Title. II. Series.
  DS254.75.K49 2011
  955—dc22
                            2010036239

Chelsea House books are available at special discounts when purchased in bulk quantities for businesses, associations, institutions, or sales promotions. Please call our Special Sales Department in New York at (212) 967-8800 or (800) 322-8755.

You can find Chelsea House on the World Wide Web at
http://www.chelseahouse.com

Text design by Takeshi Takahashi
Cover design by Alicia Post
Composition by EJB Publishing Services
Cover printed by Yurchak Printing, Landisville, Penn.
Book printed and bound by Yurchak Printing, Landisville, Penn.
Date printed April 2011
Printed in the United States of America

10 9 8 7 6 5 4 3 2 1

This book is printed on acid-free paper.

All links and Web addresses were checked and verified to be correct at the time of publication. Because of the dynamic nature of the Web, some addresses and links may have changed since publication and may no longer be valid.

Table of Contents

Iran
Second Edition

Iran is a country with a rich history. Today, much of the nation's cultural heritage coexists with modern development. Above, a modern café below the Si-o-se Pol (the bridge of 33 arches) allows patrons to enjoy the historic Zayandeh Rud (Life-Giving River), on whose banks a prehistoric culture lived in the fifth millennium B.C.

1

Introducing
Iran

Once a great world civilization, Iran still is one of the most fascinating nations of the modern world. It is also one of the world's most misunderstood countries. The political upheaval following the 1979 revolution created an image of Iran throughout the Western world that was characterized by religious fanaticism, terrorism, and anti-Americanism. This image, though partially accurate, by no means represents the true nature of Iran and Iranians. As a matter of fact, up to the time of the revolution, Iran was a close friend of the United States. American presidents and officials frequently visited Iran and spent their vacations there. American advisers and consultants were seen all over the country, advising the government, the military, and industrial and other private enterprises.

Due to its breathtaking natural beauty and its rich cultural heritage, Iran was also a popular tourist destination for Americans and other tourists from different parts of the world. The country's physical beauty and cultural and historical sites still attract a large number of international tourists. The appealing warm waters of the Caspian Sea, the lush green forests of northern Iran, the majestic snow-capped summits of the Elburz Mountains, and the esoteric marshes and deserts of the central Iranian Plateau provide Iran with one of the world's most diverse natural landscapes.

Iran's unique physical geography has made it a land of four seasons, where at any chosen time, a visitor can feel all four seasons by moving throughout the country. In northwestern Iran, people can take refuge from the chilly winds of the winter or ski on the snow-covered mountain slopes. At the same time, in the warm waters of the Persian Gulf in southern Iran, others can swim and water-ski to cool off from the heat of the day. The barren desert lands of central Iran also offer a sharp contrast to the dense forests covering much of northern Iran.

Iran is located at a "crossroads of civilizations." This historical factor, combined with its central location within the Middle East, gives the country considerable geopolitical importance. Historically, its central location has made possible regular contact between Iranians and neighboring cultures. Its rich natural resources have attracted many invading armies that have sought to control the nation during various periods of Iran's extensive history. The discovery of fossil fuels (petroleum, natural gas, and coal) at the beginning of the twentieth century also brought first the British and later the Americans to Iran.

Iran is the only country that has access to two of the world's richest deposits of oil and natural gas—the Persian Gulf and Caspian Sea basin. Iran currently holds 9 to 10 percent of the world's total petroleum reserves and is among the largest producers and exporters of oil in the world. Iran also contains the second-largest amount of natural gas deposits in the world, after Russia. It is estimated that the country owns 15 percent of

Located along ancient East–West trade routes and home to vast natural resources of its own, Iran has long held a position of importance. The discovery of abundant fossil fuels in the early twentieth century made Iran an important trading partner for industrialized nations such as Britain and the United States. Iran currently holds just under 10 percent of the world's oil.

the world's natural gas. Fossil fuels have become the lifeblood of the industrial world, and Iran is a major contributor due to its vast energy resources.

Oil is not, however, Iran's only contribution to the world. In more than 2,500 years of written history, its people have contributed to the development of global civilization in many ways. Iran has enriched world civilization in the areas of religion, science, art, literature, and politics. Iran provided the world with the prophet Zoroaster, who lived sometime during the seventh or sixth century B.C., and who was founder of the Zoroastrian religion, long before Jesus and Muhammad. Zoroastrianism was the first religion that introduced humanity to religious concepts such as angels, heaven, and hell, concepts that were later borrowed by Christianity. The origin of the word *paradise* comes from the Old Persian language. Later leaders of various Persian empires promoted Zoroaster's teachings, which declared that salvation comes through following the principle of "Good Deeds, Good Words, and Good Thoughts."

Iran also gave the world its first major empire. The Persian Empire, as it was known, predated the Greek Empire that was established by Alexander the Great. At its peak under Darius the Great, the empire stretched from the Indus Valley to the Nile Valley and northwestward to the Danube River. Cyrus the Great, who founded the empire, liberated the Jews from many years of living in captivity when he defeated the Babylonian Empire to the west in 539 B.C. The Bible, in the book of Isaiah, refers to Cyrus the Great as the liberator of the Jews. Many Jews who chose to remain in Persian territories are ancestors of the current Iranian Jewish population.

Iran is a land of linguistic, ethnic, and religious diversity. Even though Persian is the official language of modern Iran, other languages and dialects are spoken throughout the country. In addition to being multilingual, Iran is also ethnically diverse. Although Persians form the majority of the population, other groups residing in Iran include Turks, Arabs, Kurds, and Baluchis. Due to a long history of coexistence among these different ethnic groups, modern Iranians are of mixed ancestry. One cannot easily distinguish the ethnicity of a particular individual by appearance alone.

It is not uncommon for a traveler to notice churches, synagogues, and Zoroastrian temples while driving in Tehran and some other Iranian cities. Although several religions are practiced today, most Iranians are Muslims. Islam was introduced in Iran by an invading Arab army during the seventh century A.D. Soon after its introduction, however, Islam became a popular religion among Iranians. Many converted to the new faith and embraced the ideals of Islam. The simplicity, the inherent social justice, and the egalitarianism (equality) of Islam attracted many Iranians who were dissatisfied with the former stratified social system sanctified by corrupt religious leaders.

During the sixteenth century, the Safavid dynasty made the Shiite branch of Islam Iran's official religion, and Iran is now the largest Shiite Muslim country in the world. Gathering under the banner of Shiism, the country became united and was able to resist the expansionist tendencies of the emerging Turkish Ottoman Empire to the west. During the history of Shiism in Iran, however, Shiite clerics never controlled the national government until the emergence of the Islamic Republic of Iran in 1979.

This book will take you on a multidimensional tour of Iran. You will travel through time and space as you visit this fascinating land and visit with its varied people and places. We will begin with a journey through Iran's diverse physical landscapes.

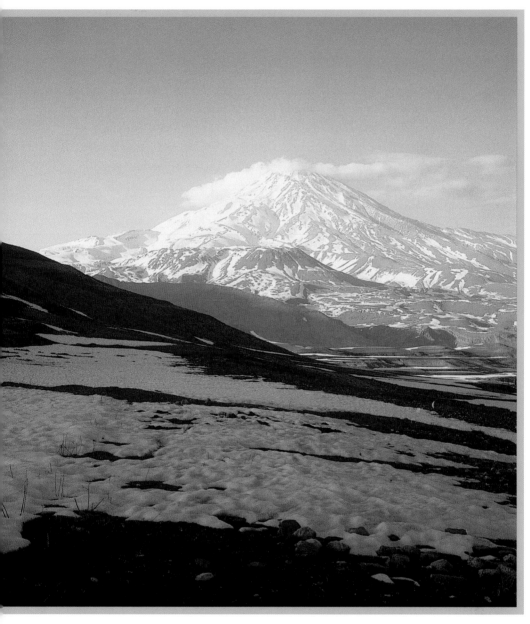

Standing over 18,600 feet (5,671 meters) above sea level, Mount Damavand with its snow-capped volcanic cone is among the most picturesque mountains in the world.

2

Physical Landscapes

Extending between 25 and 40 degrees north latitude and 44 and 63 degrees east longitude, Iran covers an area about twice the size of the U.S. states of California, Oregon, and Washington combined. With an area of some 636,296 square miles (1,648,000 square kilometers), it is also three times the size of France.

Situated in the heart of the Middle East in southwest Asia, Iran is a bridge linking Asia and Europe. To the north, Iran shares borders with three newly independent republics: Armenia, Azerbaijan, and Turkmenistan. Prior to their independence, the former Soviet Union controlled all three. To the north, Iran also borders the Caspian Sea, the world's largest landlocked body of water. Due to its being land-locked, the Caspian Sea is officially considered a lake rather than a sea; however, due to its large size, historically it has been referred to as a sea. To the south, Iran borders the Persian Gulf and the Gulf of

Oman. It shares its eastern border with Afghanistan and Pakistan and its western border with Turkey and Iraq.

At their border, Iran and Iraq share a major body of water formed by the joining of major rivers that pour into the Persian Gulf. The Tigris and Euphrates rivers flowing in Iraq join the Karun River flowing in Iran to form the strategically significant body of water called Shatt al-Arab (Arabian River) by Iraqis and Arvand Rud (River Arvand) by Iranians. Due to its periodic meandering, the stream has been a source of boundary disputes between the two countries. One of the major objectives of the Iraqi government's invasion of Iran in September 1980 was the annexation of this strategic and economically important body of water.

TOPOGRAPHY AND EARTHQUAKES

As mentioned, Iran is located between two major depressions, the Caspian Sea to the north and the Persian Gulf to the south. A series of mountains rising steeply from these depressions, along with other isolated mountain chains, forms a high outer rim that encloses the interior basin. This configuration provides Iran with an overall bowl-shaped topography that characterizes the country's general physical appearance. The interior basin is known as the Iranian Plateau. According to geologists, the plateau is an ancient former seabed that took its present shape during the Quaternary period about 200,000 years ago. It was formed and shaped by the uplifting and folding effects of three giant plates pressing against each other. The interacting plates are the Arabian Plate, the Eurasian Plate, and the Indian Plate. The continuous process of squeezing and pressing resulted in a considerable folding at the edges, and some folding in the interior, which eventually formed Iran's present mountain ranges.

The continuing geologic process of uplifting and folding is also responsible for earthquakes—subterranean shifts in the earth that take place near the numerous fault zones formed by the movement of the plates. About 90 percent of Iran falls within an active seismic (earthquake-prone) zone. Most of the country is subject to the tremors and the devastation that they can cause. On December 26, 2003, a major earthquake (with 6.6 Richter force) hit the ancient central Iranian city of Bam and surrounding areas, destroying the city, killing about 30,000 people, and injuring more than 70,000 others. The year before, on June 22, 2002, a major earthquake hit the northwestern region of Iran, causing significant damage and casualties to small mountain towns and villages in the area. The earthquake, with a force of 6.4 on the Richter scale, was felt as far away as Tehran, approximately 180 miles (290 kilometers) east of the epicenter. The death toll was 261, and the number of injured exceeded 1,300 people. In addition, more than 25,000 people were left homeless. Many villages were totally destroyed, and many others lost their water supply as a result of this earthquake.

A much more devastating earthquake occurred earlier, on June 21, 1990, in northern Iran. It caused 50,000 deaths, 100,000 injuries, and left 500,000 homeless. Other major earthquakes during recent decades have claimed the lives of many Iranian people. For example, a 1997 earthquake in eastern Iran with a magnitude of 7.1 on the Richter scale killed 2,000 people and destroyed 200 villages. Another quake, measuring 7.7, occurred in 1978 in the eastern province of Khorasan. It killed 25,000 people and completely destroyed the ancient city of Tabas along with a large number of villages. The cheaply built adobe (mud-brick) buildings are the main reason for the vast destruction and high death tolls. When they collapse, people and everything else inside can easily be crushed.

TOPOGRAPHY AND WATER

The peculiar topography of Iran, particularly the orientation of mountains, has resulted in the country's general aridity. With the exception of two strips in the northern and western sections of the country, Iran consists mainly of dry lands

Iran is located between two major depressions, the Caspian Sea to the north and the Persian Gulf to the south. It shares borders with Pakistan and Afghanistan to the east, Turkey and Iraq to the west, and Turkmenistan, Azerbaijan, and Armenia to the north.

and barren mountains. The rugged Elburz Mountains, which stretch in a general northwest–southeast direction along the southern shores of the Caspian Sea, block the moist northerly winds coming from the Caspian Sea and result in an uneven distribution of precipitation over the plateau. By the same token, the Zagros Mountains, extending from the northwest to the southeast of Iran, stand in the way of rain-bearing westerly winds coming from the Mediterranean Sea. Therefore, while the windward mountain slopes receive a considerable amount of moisture, the downwind central basins of the plateau receive very little precipitation.

The Elburz range contains numerous peaks rising above 12,000 feet (3,658 meters). Northeast of Tehran, Iran's highest peak, snow-capped Mount Damavand, reaches an elevation of 18,605 feet (5,671 meters). With its impressive symmetrical volcanic cone, Mount Damavand is one of the world's most majestic and picturesque summits. The steep northern slopes of the Elburz Mountains fall sharply from more than 10,000-foot (3,048-meter) summits to the Caspian shores, which lie about 90 feet (27.5 meters) below sea level.

The amount of precipitation varies from more than 50 inches (127 centimeters) on the Caspian coast to less than 2 inches (5 centimeters) in the desert areas. The central plateau, consisting of closed basins with an average elevation of 300 feet (90 meters), forms the most arid region of Iran. The annual rainfall here is less than 4 inches (10 centimeters), and the relative humidity rarely exceeds 20 percent. The most significant basins within the central plateau are the two salt deserts known as Dasht-e Kavir and Dasht-e Lut (*dasht* means "open land" in Persian). These barren regions are among the world's most inhospitable deserts, with their whitish salt crust, hot summer days, cold winters, and black, muddy marshes.

Mountain barriers (to prevailing winds) have resulted in a stunning contrast between relatively green slopes facing the incoming moist air and the barren slopes on the opposite sides that form the parched "rain shadow" slopes. This contrast shows clearly in the distribution and settlement of the population throughout the country.

WATER AND SETTLEMENTS

The availability of water has always played a major role in the distribution and intensity of human activity in Iran. Most settlements occur on the sides of the mountains with access to water. For example, eastward-moving air coming from the Mediterranean Sea carries enough moisture to support a significant population in the western regions of Iran, mainly along the western slopes of the Zagros Mountains. These incoming moist air currents provide a relatively steady supply of surface water for some intermountain basins where cities such as Tabriz, Hamadan, Kermanshah, Shiraz, and Esfahan (Isfahan) are located. The availability of water also allows green pastures that support livestock grazing.

Several rivers originate at high elevations in the Zagros Mountains. These streams bring prosperity and physical attractiveness to the cities they irrigate. For example, the city of Esfahan, with its large area beyond the city, is irrigated by the Zayandeh Rud (Life-Giving River), which provides a fascinating focal point for the city. Other rivers, such as the Karun, Karkheh, and Dez, originate from the highlands of the Zagros Mountains, irrigate the fertile plain of Khuzestan in the southwest region of the country, and pass through large cities such as Dezful, Shushtar, Ahwaz, and Abadan.

Similarly, moist northerly winds blowing from over the Caspian Sea come in contact with the high Elburz Mountains and cause enough precipitation to support a sizable population along the northern slopes of the range and on the coastal lowlands bordering the Caspian Sea. The two provinces of Mazanderan and Gilan, located along the lower northern slopes of the Elburz, are among the most densely populated provinces of Iran. Cities located to the south of the Elburz Mountains, on the central plateau, receive much less precipitation. Tehran, for example, is located at an elevation of about 5,000 feet (1,500 meters) at the southern base of the Elburz. The city, Iran's largest, cannot survive without the use of an extensive aquifer (underground water).

The coastal lowlands receive a considerable amount of rainfall year-round and are the most suitable lands for crop production. These lowlands receive runoff from the northern slopes of the Elburz Mountains, from such large streams as the Safid Rud, Haraz, Babol, Tejan, and Gorgan. Due to this availability of water, the area is the most suitable place for production of crops such as tea and rice—the main staple in the diet of the Iranian people. Among the cities located on these lowlands are Rasht (near the Safid Rud), Sary (along the Tejan River), Babol (on the bank of the Babol River), and Gorgan (on the Gorgan River).

There is no permanent river on the central plateau. Streams that reach the central plateau have dry beds for much of the year. During the spring, when mountain snow begins to melt, rivers begin to flow into salt lakes. But during the hot summer, these rivers dry up, as do most of the salt lakes into which they flow. Lake Urumia (also known as Rezaiyeh) is the most important permanent salt lake. It is located in the northwestern province of Azerbaijan (though it has the same name, this region is separate from the independent republic of Azerbaijan, located north of Iran and which was part of the former Soviet Union). Because of its high salinity and mineral content, Lake Urumia cannot support fish or any other aquatic life. It is, however, a main tourist attraction due to its natural beauty and its reputation that its water is able to cure various skin problems.

QANATS

Many areas bordering the central deserts receive fewer than 8 inches (20 centimeters) of annual precipitation, which is inadequate for dry (nonirrigated) agriculture. A traveler to Iran,

The Caspian Sea is the largest landlocked body of water in the world, making it a giant lake. Unlike the remainder of the nation, the Caspian Sea region receives ample annual rainfall, and the sea's warm waters make it a popular destination for visitors.

however, would be surprised to see many Iranian cities located along these fringes. How do these cities meet their water needs? An answer was found in an ancient technological innovation known in Iran as the *qanat*.

Qanats are subterranean aqueducts. Rainwater falling on the uplands runs off the bedrock and partly seeps into the gravel and sands at the base of the mountains, gathering in underground reservoirs. Qanats collect this fresh groundwater and carry it by gravity flow through gently sloping under-ground aqueducts (tunnels) to faraway settlements. Because qanats are often the only source of water, the distribution of settlements in the desert margins of Iran is closely related to the distribution of the qanat systems.

Winds also play a major role in the absence of cities in Iran's central desert. Winds affecting central Iran often carry with them sand and dust, so they damage crops and livestock, cover roads and houses, and continually change the surface features of the land. For example, the *baad-e sad-o-bist roozeh* (Wind of 120 Days), which originates over the central deserts during summer days, is hot and violent, carrying abrasive sand particles. With a velocity that can reach 70 miles (110 kilometers) per hour, it blows toward the provinces of Sistan and Baluchistan, destroying plants and vegetation, stripping away the soil, and damaging buildings and livestock.

Although the physical geography of the Iranian Plateau has a significant impact on the location of Iranian cities, it alone does not account for the presence or absence of settlements. One cannot ignore cultural factors, such as major trade routes, military and strategic requirements, and religious and political considerations.

CLIMATE AND VEGETATION COVER

Iran has the most diverse climate of all Middle Eastern countries. It varies from subtropical in the south to subpolar at high elevations. During winter, a high-pressure belt develops over Siberia. Its clear, often bone-chilling weather moves west and south to reach the interior basin of the Iranian Plateau. In contrast to this cold Siberian air, the warm waters of the Persian Gulf, Caspian Sea, and Mediterranean help to develop low-pressure systems over these waters. When these conflicting pressure systems meet, the dynamics exist for local wind formation.

The northwest is the coldest region of Iran. It is known for its cold winters with heavy snows and below freezing winter temperatures. Summers in this region, however, are dry and hot, with spring and fall being relatively mild and pleasant. The south, particularly near the Persian Gulf, is known for its unpleasant climate. It has very hot and humid summers, with temperatures that have reached 123°F (50.5°C) in

Khuzestan Province at the head of the gulf. The high humidity, accompanied by the excessive heat in this region, makes the weather almost unbearable for people from other parts of the country who are not used to it. Due to these harsh climatic conditions, people from Tehran, for example, who are asked by their companies to work in this region receive higher salaries than their counterparts working in Tehran. Winters, however, are mild and are the best time to visit this area.

The Persian Gulf area, with its scorching heat and energy-sapping humidity, stands in sharp contrast to the Caspian coastal region to the north. In the Caspian region, moist air from the sea mingles with dry air currents from the Elburz Mountains and creates a pleasant nighttime breeze. The appealing warm water of the sea, accompanied by the pleasantly cool climate and beautiful natural landscape, has made the Caspian Sea coastal areas popular tourist destinations.

The Caspian Sea region also receives the country's greatest amount of precipitation. In the high mountain valleys, the annual precipitation reaches as much as 80 inches (203 centimeters). The amount of precipitation is also distributed evenly throughout the year in this area. In contrast, with the exception of the high mountain valleys of the Zagros and Caspian coastal plain, precipitation throughout the rest of the country is relatively scant, and usually falls from October through April. The annual average precipitation for the country as a whole is about 14 inches (36 centimeters).

Roughly speaking, only about 10 percent of Iran is forested. While there are lush forests covering the northern slopes of the Elburz Mountains, the rest of the country has few forested areas. For example, the central deserts of Iran receive only a few inches of precipitation each year. The scant moisture does not allow soil formation or much vegetation growth. In the Caspian region, the most common vegetation patterns are thorny shrubs and ferns and broad-leafed deciduous trees, usually oak, beech, linden, elm, walnut, and ash, as well as a few broad-leafed evergreens.

In the Zagros Mountains, one finds semi-humid oak forests, together with elm, maple, walnut, pear, and pistachio. In the ravines, one can find trees including willow and poplar, as well as many species of creepers. In the semi-dry plateau, thin stands of juniper, almond, and wild fruit trees are found. Steppes are covered by grasses and thorny shrubs, while acacia and dwarf palms often grow in areas below 3,000 feet (914 meters). In oases, one can see tamarisk, poplar, date palm, myrtle, oleander, acacia, willow, elm, plum, and mulberry trees, as well as vines. Reeds and grass provide good pasture in swamp areas.

CLIMATE AND THE CITY

With the exception of the two narrow regions bordering the Caspian Sea and the western slopes of the Zagros Mountains, Iran is an arid country. It is characterized by shortage of water, higher evaporation than precipitation, and low relative humidity. It also experiences intense solar radiation during hot summer days, high daily and seasonal temperature ranges, torrential (but sporadic) spurts of precipitation, and damaging sandstorms and dust storms. Through centuries of coping with these climatic conditions, Iranians learned to build their settlements in a way to minimize the impact of solar radiation and harmful and unpleasant winds and to optimize shade, breeze, and water.

Traditional cities adopted a compact urban form that included narrow winding streets, buildings set close together, houses with courtyard ponds, covered bazaars, and wind-capturing towers. The compact city form minimizes the empty space that can become a source of heat during the day and cold at night. The narrow winding streets provide shade for passersby and protect them from sand- and dust-laden storms. The courtyard ponds provide the surrounding rooms with cool air through evaporation. Wind towers harness air to cool off the rooms below. The covered bazaar protects shoppers from rain and allows cool air to circulate.

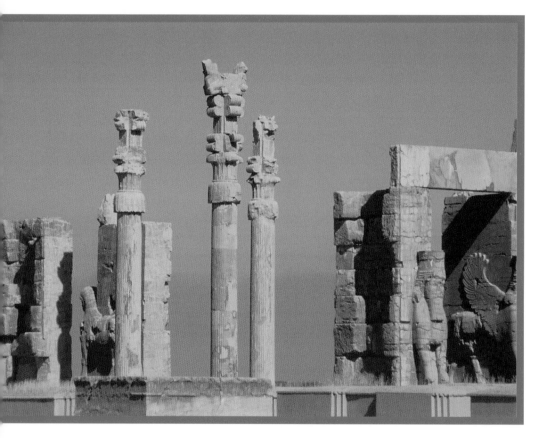

Built in 512 B.C., Persepolis was the center for ceremonies and worship during the ancient Achaemenid Empire, which lasted from 550 to 330 B.C. This great empire was established by Cyrus the Great. Later, under Darius the Great, the empire stretched from India to the Nile River. Darius ordered the construction of a magnificent palace at Persepolis that can still be seen in these ruins today.

3

Iran
Through Time

What we call Iran today is part of a much greater geographical area that once was home to a very highly developed culture and a great civilization. Today, traces of Iranian culture can be seen outside modern Iranian borders in places such as Pakistan, Afghanistan, central Asia, the Caucasus, eastern Turkey, Iraq, and the southern Persian Gulf coastal region. These are all areas that historically were part of the Persian Empire and therefore were influenced by Persian culture. Iranians tend to refer to the realm of Iranian cultural influence as "Iran Zamin," meaning, in the Persian language, "the Land of Iran."

The term *Iran* is a derivative of the word *Aryan* ("the noble"). Iranians were a branch of Aryan tribes who entered Iran from central Asia sometime during the second millennium B.C. and settled in the western and south-central parts of what is now modern Iran.

While Aryans are believed to be the ancestors of modern Iranians, there were many other groups who lived in Iran before their arrival in the region. As a matter of fact, the history of the earliest sedentary cultures, based on existing archaeological sites, can be traced back some 18,000 years. And evidence suggests that humans occupied the region as long ago as 100,000 years.

IRAN OR PERSIA?

Today, confusion exists among many Westerners on the proper use of the terms Iran, Iranian, Persia, and Persian. What are the differences in meaning? The terms Iran and Persia are used interchangeably, because both refer to the same land. Persia was the name the Greeks used when they spoke of Iran. The origin of the term comes from the word *pars,* or *parsa,* the heart of the great Persian Empire, where today's Iranian province of Pars, or Fars, is located. So, Persian simply means Parsi, or people of Persia.

Iranians, however, have always referred to their land as Iran and considered themselves to be Iranians. In 1935, the government officially registered the country's name as Iran and demanded that the international community so recognize it. This way Iran could be remembered as the continuation of the Iran Zamin (the "Land of Iran") founded and expanded by the Iranian ancestors, the Aryans.

PRE-ISLAMIC HISTORY

Aryans were nomadic people in search of better land when they entered the Iranian Plateau toward the end of the second millennium B.C. The reason for their migration may have been that they exhausted the natural resources, such as croplands and pastures, in their homeland. A group of these immigrants settled along the western slopes of the Zagros Mountains and set the foundation for an emerging empire known in the West as the Achaemenid Empire. Most of Iran's present-day nomads, still living on the slopes of these rugged mountains, are descendants of the original Aryans.

ACHAEMENID EMPIRE (550–330 B.C.)

The Achaemenid Empire, known also as the Persian Empire, became one of the greatest empires the world had ever seen. It was established by Cyrus the Great, who defeated the powerful Babylonian Empire in 539 B.C. While in Babylon, Cyrus ordered the release of Jewish prisoners who had lived in captivity for many years. For this he became known as the "liberator of Jews," as is revealed in Jewish history and as is documented in the book of Isaiah in the Old Testament. The empire that Cyrus created reached its peak during the reign of Darius the Great (541–486 B.C.). Under Darius, the empire stretched from the western borders of modern India to the valley of the Nile River and included numerous satellite kingdoms.

Darius is called "a great statesman" in the Bible. For the first time in history, he ordered the use of coins in trade. The use of gold and silver coinage later revolutionized economic exchange and world trade. Achaemenid rulers constructed substantial highway systems and pioneered advanced irrigation techniques. They also codified commercial laws, created a universal legal system, devised a universal system of weights and measures, and developed a reliable mail and postage system. Today's U.S. Postal Service motto (used also back in the days of the Pony Express) that "neither snow, rain, heat, nor gloom of night" will stop the mail from its delivery is modeled after a motto originated by the Achaemenids.

Building the necessary infrastructure (physical links such as roads) facilitated trade and communication throughout the satellite territories and paved the way for further expansion of the empire. With trade came the diffusion (spread) of a new culture and ideas. Some of the Persian words for typical items of trade became widely used throughout the empire. Later, some of these words entered the English language. Persian was the official language of the empire used for inscriptions and proclamations; however, the more commonly used language throughout the empire was Aramaic.

Art and architecture also flourished during the reign of the Achaemenids. As a result of their extensive contact with the far reaches of the empire, the kings employed skilled artisans and professionals from different cultural groups, including religious groups, to work on major projects, such as Persepolis, the winter capital of the Archaemenid Empire. Today, the impressive remains of Persepolis, located north of the modern city of Shiraz in south-central Iran, testify to the magnificent glory of Iran's past.

The Achaemenid Empire fell to the emerging Greek Empire of Alexander the Great. To humiliate his defeated rival, Alexander burned the beautiful city of Persepolis when he defeated the last king of the empire in 330 B.C. Alexander, however, was soon taken by the richness of Iranian culture and found the fusion of Greek and Iranian culture a noble idea. He married Roxana (Roshanak), a Persian princess, and encouraged 10,000 of his soldiers to marry Iranian women. A mass wedding in the city of Susa, ordered by Alexander, displayed his desire to complete the union of the Greeks and Iranians.

SELEUCIDS AND PARTHIANS

After the sudden death of Alexander in 323 B.C., at the age of 32, one of his generals ruled over most of the former Persian Empire and established a dynasty known as the Seleucids. During the Seleucids, Hellenistic art, architecture, and urban planning began to diffuse into Iranian territories, and Iranian culture was enriched by incorporation of Greek cultural traits.

In 247 B.C., however, Iranians revolted against the Greek Seleucids and established a dynasty known as Parthians. Parthians, who claimed ancestry from both Persians and Greeks, managed to retrieve a good portion of the former empire. They

In A.D. 224, Ardeshir overthrew the last king of the Parthian dynasty and established the Sassanid dynasty, which endured for more than 400 years. In this relief, Ardeshir is seen receiving his crown from the god Ahura Mazda.

adopted an administrative system similar to that of the Achaemenids and used the Persian language and a form of writing called Pahlavi script as their official language.

In A.D. 224, the last king of the Parthian dynasty was overthrown by Ardeshir, a rival power who claimed descent from the Achaemenids. Ardeshir, the son of Sassan, then established the Sassanid dynasty that lasted for more than 400 years.

SASSANIDS (A.D. 224–642)

Early Sassanid kings were capable rulers. They expanded their empire to the extent that it became roughly equal in area to that of the Achaemenids. The city of Ctesiphon (in present-day Iraq) was their capital. Their rulers adopted the title of shahanshah, meaning the "the king of kings" in Persian. Sassanids are known for improving the quality of life in cities and for developments in agriculture and technology.

Under the Sassanids, the administrative system became more centralized, the tax system was reformed, and the army was reorganized to tie the military more closely to the central government than to local lords. New towns were built, and education and health care were improved. Scholars were encouraged to translate books from other languages into Pahlavi, the language of the empire. Many of these books, especially those brought from India, later became popular reading throughout the Islamic world.

The structure of society consisted of four major classes: priests, warriors, secretaries, and commoners. This stratified system gave privileges to princes, petty rulers, priests, and landlords, and deprived both artisans and peasants. The system was sanctioned and supported by the Zoroastrian priests, who became immensely powerful in the court of Sassanid leaders. Zoroastrianism became the empire's official religion.

At this time Iran's archenemies were the Byzantines (Eastern Romans), whose capital was Constantinople (present-day Istanbul, Turkey). Toward the end of the Sassanid Empire, too many wars with the Byzantines had exhausted and weakened both sides. During the last years of the dynasty, the empire was characterized by economic decline, heavy taxation, religious unrest, rigid social stratification, the increasing power of provincial landlords, and a rapid turnover of rulers. These problems facilitated the Arab takeover in the seventh century.

ISLAMIC PERIOD

During the seventh century A.D., an invading Arab Islamic army defeated the Sassanids and introduced Islam to Iran. Up to this point, most Iranians had been Zoroastrians, the official religion of the empire. Zoroastrian church leaders acted as the moral supporters of kings and their policies. In this way, kings legitimized their power through support of religious leaders.

The Islamic army, which already had defeated the mighty Byzantines at Damascus, Syria, defeated the weak and demoralized Sassanid army in A.D. 641. Iranian soldiers, mainly recruited from peasant families, did not see an urgent need to protect their homes against the Arabs. They had already heard about the egalitarian (equality) message of Islam and assumed that a government ruled under the Islamic principle of justice would be better than the morally corrupt government of recent Sassanid rulers. Thus, soon after its introduction, Islam became a popular religion among Iranians. Many converted to the new religion and embraced its ideals. Its simplicity and message of social justice and egalitarianism attracted many Iranians who were dissatisfied with the socially stratified system of the Sassanid Empire promoted by corrupt religious leaders.

Another factor that sped up the conversion process was the fact that Arab rulers provided tax relief to those converting to Islam. Islam soon began replacing the Zoroastrian religion in many Iranian cities. It took until the ninth century, however, before the majority of Iranians had become Muslims, as followers of Islam are called.

The Arab conquerors, like other past invaders, soon embraced many elements of Iranian culture and adopted some of the Sassanid administrative practices. Among them were the office of vizier ("minister" in the Persian language); the divan, a bureau for controlling state revenues and expenditures; and court ceremonial practices. Many Iranians served as administrators and ministers at the courts of Arab caliphs (leaders).

Islamic conquests under the Arab rulers brought many new territories under the control of the Arab caliphs, and Islam became the ideological blueprint of a vast Muslim empire that matched those of the Achaemenids and Sassanids. A high degree of tolerance for religious, ethnic, and cultural diversity created a very successful empire known for its achievements in art, science, and technology.

Iranian intellectuals played a major role in developing the Islamic civilization. They contributed to the development of many branches of Islamic learning, such as theology, philosophy, literature, jurisprudence, medicine, science, history, and geography. Although Arabic was chosen to be the official language of the court in A.D. 696, Persian remained the spoken language throughout most of the Iranian cultural region. The Persian language, however, adopted the Arabic script and borrowed many Arab words during Arab rule.

As had happened to other rulers in the past, the Arabs gradually lost control over the vast Iranian territory. Several local dynasties with central Asian origins challenged the Arab rule, gaining control over different regions. There was also infighting among these groups, and some came to be more powerful than others. Among the more significant dynasties of this period were the Samanids (875–1005), Ghaznavids (962–1186), and Seljuks (1037–1220). The cultural and scientific achievements during the Seljuk reign were significant. Under the leadership of Nizam al-Mulk, the popular Iranian vizier, many schools, universities, and observatories were built. In one of these observatories, Omar Khayyam, the well-known poet and mathematician, conducted much of his experimentation leading to the creation of a new calendar. The Seljuk rule, however, came to an end when the Mongols invaded Iran.

MONGOL INVASION

The Mongol invasion left a bitter legacy throughout Iran. Genghis (Chingiz in Persian) Khan devastated whatever city he passed through and killed a large number of Iranian people between 1220 and 1258. Mongol soldiers even destroyed the qanat (subterranean aqueduct) systems and made food production difficult throughout the region.

In 1258, Mongols captured Baghdad, the capital of the dynasty of the Abbasids, and by killing the last caliph, ended Arab rule in the region. Life improved, however, during the later Mongol rulers. Under Ghazan Khan and his Iranian vizier, Rashid ad Din Fazlullah, the economy revived, taxes were lowered, irrigation systems were built or repaired, and international trade improved. Due to an increase in commerce with China and India, Iran was more exposed to the art and culture of these great nations. For example, the Chinese influence in Persian paintings made Chinese-style miniatures popular in Iran.

Tamerlane, another ruthless Mongol, emerged as a world power when he conquered central Asia. Like Genghis Khan, he invaded Iran and destroyed many cities, including Shiraz and Esfahan. Tamerlane, however, had a soft side. Later, during his reign, he became a patron of art and promoted architects and poets. His successors also built many mosques and religious schools. The Mongol rule came to its end when the Safavid dynasty emerged as a major power.

SAFAVIDS (1501–1722)

Since the invasion of Iran by the Arab army in 641, the Safavids were the first true Iranian dynasty to rule the country. The Safavids came to power in 1501 when they captured the city of Tabriz (in the northwestern province of Azerbaijan) and made it their capital. From there, they expanded their rule over territories as extensive as those of the Sassanids.

The Safavids claimed to be direct descendents of the seventh Shiite Imam, Musa al-Kazim. They thus legitimized their power through their connection to the family of Muhammad, the Prophet of Islam. The Safavids declared Shiite Islam as the official religion of the state and recruited people, using force when necessary, to convert to the Shiite sect (Shiism). The Safavids at first managed their government as a semi-theocracy (a government strongly influenced by religion). Kings considered themselves spiritual as well as political leaders. During the reign of later kings such as Shah Abbas the Great (1587–1629), religion and state, however, began to distance themselves from each other.

Kings established a strong fighting force known as *qizil-bash*, whose members were chosen from mainly Turkish-speaking tribes. Their rivals were the mighty Ottomans to the west. The Ottoman Empire—the Turkish Muslim empire with its capital in present-day Istanbul—was expanding in all directions. It managed to capture Iraq from the Safavids and was fighting battles over the control of Azerbaijan and the Caucasus. In 1639, the Safavids and Ottomans signed a peace treaty that established frontiers in both Iraq and the Caucasus. Those borders are still in effect between Iran and its western neighboring states.

Shah Abbas changed the Safavid capital from Tabriz to Esfahan. He and his successors showed a great interest in making Esfahan a showcase of architecture and city planning. By building several magnificent mosques, religious schools, bazaars, and palaces, Shah Abbas wanted Esfahan to surpass the Ottoman capital of Istanbul in grandeur and beauty.

Besides being a true patron of art, Shah Abbas also promoted commerce. He worked closely with the British to expel the Portuguese from Bahrain and the island of Hormuz in the Persian Gulf. He encouraged European powers to do business with Iran. There was a great increase and improvement in the production of fine silks, carpets, cloths, and metalware.

Safavid power, however, declined during the reign of its last two rulers due to corruption, rivalries among army officers, mismanagement of state revenues and land, excessive taxation, decline in trade, and the weakening of the military

Naqsh-e Jahan Square ("Image of the World Square") or as it is called in Iran 'maidaan-e naqsh-e Jahan' was built during the Safavids. It is a huge square about 1,667 feet (508 meters) long and 525 (160 meters) wide. The square is one the most attractive Iranian historic sites located at the center of Isfahan.

organization. In 1722, the last Safavid king submitted to an Afghan tribal leader who invaded Iran and captured Esfahan.

Afghan rule over Iran was short-lived. In 1736, Nader Shah defeated the Afghan army and established the Afshar dynasty. A powerful military leader, Nader Shah also defeated the Otto-mans in Georgia and Armenia and the Russians on the Caspian

Sea coasts and restored territories controlled by the Safavids. He also took his army to India and defeated Indian rulers and brought back many treasures. Nader Shah's rule was followed by a period of anarchy during which many groups competed for power. Karim Khan (1750–1779) succeeded in overcoming rivals and establishing the Zand dynasty. Karim Khan refused to accept the title of shah, insisting that he was a servant of the people, rather than a king. History remembers him most for his kind rule.

QAJARS (1795–1925)

The Qajars took over Iran after they defeated the last Zand ruler in 1794. They moved their seat of government from Esfahan to Tehran, a city that continues to serve as Iran's capital. After overcoming the challenges to their power from tribal chiefs, they brought a relative degree of unity, peace, and tranquility to Iran during their earlier years. Qajar rulers (shahs) referred to themselves as the "shadow of God on earth," and by gathering the Shiite religious leaders around them, they further legitimized their rule over their subjects. They were absolute rulers and appointed different princes as heads of the states and provinces and established a large bureaucracy.

But during the Qajar reign, the Iranian economy was suffering, the bureaucracy and army were in disorder, and the government was very corrupt. Some rulers tried to improve the country's overall condition. For example, they attempted to strengthen the administration by reforming the tax system and asserting more control over the overwhelming bureaucracy at different levels of the government. They promoted trade and industrialization. They established new technological schools and invited foreign instructors to share their knowledge with young Iranians. They even reduced the influence of the clergy, who opposed modernization processes.

The Qajars also established a European-style cabinet with administrative responsibilities and a consultative council of senior princes and officials. They opened the Karun River in Khuzestan to foreign trade and opened European-style banks. Overwhelming corruption and a rising demand among the public for more freedom and the right to participate in government decisions, however, led to the 1906 Constitutional Movement.

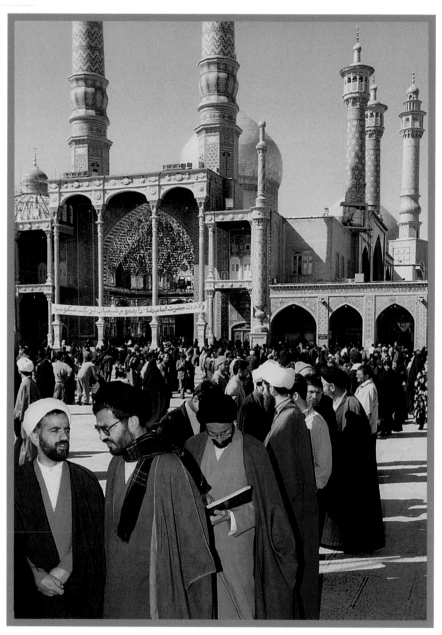

Iran is one of the world's few true theocracies—a country where political power rests in the hands of religious leaders. Here, Muslim clergymen at a shrine in Qom line up to vote in parliamentary elections.

4

Steps Toward Modern Iran

A mong the modern nations of the world, Iran is a theocratic country—one in which religious leaders hold absolute political power. Although the governments of Saudi Arabia, Libya, and Pakistan are considered to be somewhat theocratic, none are comparable to Iran. The only country with greater religious influence on its government was Afghanistan during the Taliban regime in the 1990s. The September 11, 2001, terrorist attacks on the World Trade Center in New York City and the Pentagon in Washington, D.C., which were followed by the U.S. invasion of Afghanistan, ended the Taliban regime.

Why is Iran a theocracy? Why are religion and politics so intertwined there? Perhaps the answer lies in Iran's history. Prior to the arrival of Islam in the seventh century A.D., during the Sassanid Empire, Zoroastrianism was the country's official religion.

Especially during the reign of the last Sassanid kings, religious leaders played a significant role in legitimizing the kings' rule. They were always seen working closely with the kings, supporting their national policies, eliminating rival religious groups, and in some cases imposing unjust social and economic laws.

When Islam came to Iran, the influence of religion in politics was actually increased in some ways. The fact that the Prophet Muhammad was both the spiritual leader of Islam and the political head of the Islamic community justified to Iranians the legitimacy of an Islamic state with a religious figure occupying the highest political office. Thus, throughout the Islamic history, religion and politics have been closely intertwined.

The role of Muhammad as both a politician and spiritual leader stands in sharp contrast to that of Jesus, who—at least based on what has been written about him—disliked politics and advised his followers to stick to their spiritual growth and let Romans to do the governing. This fundamental difference in the personality of these two religious leaders is a main reason for different approaches to the role religion plays in politics in modern Christian and Islamic countries. We should not ignore, however, the fact that the West went through historic events, such as the Renaissance and French Revolution, that reduced the power of the church. Similar events have not occurred in the Islamic world.

In Iran, religion and politics became more intertwined when sixteenth-century Safavid rulers announced that Shiite Islam would be the country's official religion. When Safavid rulers claimed to be descendents of Shiite Imams, whose heritage is traced to the Prophet Muhammad, they in effect legitimized their power. The Safavids claimed Iran as a safe haven for persecuted Shiites in other lands and became the champions and voice of Shiism throughout the world. Dynasties that followed the Safavids, especially the Qajars, also employed the high Shiite leaders in their courts and wanted them to support and sanction their policies and behaviors.

WESTERN INTERVENTION IN IRANIAN AFFAIRS

Beginning with colonization, the West partially met its industrial needs by expanding control over Third World lands and resources. Soon after the European voyages of discovery, European powers were competing with one another all over the world for domination of weaker lands and exploitation of their raw materials; Iran was no exception. By the nineteenth century, Iran, due to its resources and vital strategic location in the Middle East, became a pawn in a geopolitical game between the competing British and Russian empires. Being too corrupt and militarily weak, the Qajar rulers could not withstand the territorial aggression of these two superpowers.

The Russians long had sought to gain access to the warm waters of the Persian Gulf. They believed that by controlling Iran and Afghanistan, they could achieve that goal. The powerful British, however, controlled the Indian subcontinent and did not allow Russian ambitions to materialize. Qajar kings, under pressure, had to concede territory to both the Russians and British. In 1812, Russia claimed the Caucasus territories, including Armenia, Georgia, and Azerbaijan, under the Treaty of Gulistan. And with the Treaty of Turkmanchay in 1828, Russia also annexed central Asian lands from Iran. In 1857, Britain also forced Iran to give up its rights over the city of Herat and other territories in present-day Afghanistan. These two powers, especially the British, constantly interfered in Iran's internal affairs and often used existing ethnic and tribal rivalries to their advantage.

The discovery of oil in Iran and its first successful exploitation by the British in 1908 made Iran an even more attractive place to world powers. Britain controlled the Iranian oil industry until 1951, when it was nationalized.

THE EARLY CLERIC VICTORIES

Iranians disliked being ruled by despotic Qajar monarchs who were supported by European powers and often acted against the country's national interests. There were always resistance movements against foreign domination and against decisions made by kings that were not in the national interest. For example, in 1890, when a Qajar king, Nasseruddin Shah, gave a British company a complete monopoly over production and sale of tobacco, Iranians, led by religious leaders, protested the act. A religious leader, Mirza Shirazi, issued a religious decree calling for abstaining from and boycotting the use of tobacco by Muslim Iranians. The economic damage resulting from the boycott led to the cancellation of the contract. This major victory for the clergy against the autocratic kings became known as the "Tobacco Movement."

THE 1906 CONSTITUTIONAL MOVEMENT

By the end of the nineteenth century, Iranian intellectuals felt the need for a national constitution that would limit the power of the Qajar kings. People from all different walks of Iranian society, including the clergy, secular intellectuals, and merchants, supported this constitutional movement. When businessmen decided to close the bazaar, Mozaaffaru din Shah felt the economic pressure and granted Iranians their first parliament. It was known as the National Consultative Assembly, or Majlis-e Showray-e Melli. Iran thus became a constitutional monarchy, under which the monarch's power was limited and elected members of parliament made the important decisions. The Constitutional Movement is considered to be the beginning of Iranian modern history.

The Qajar leadership could not accept this loss of power, so the next king ordered the bombardment of the parliament and the arrest and execution of some parliamentary members. After this, the parliament faced uncertainty, as did the rest of the country under the remaining Qajar kings. During this period, there were many mass revolts, some for democratization of the country and others by ethnic groups seeking political autonomy. The British and the Russians, in exchange for favors, supported the corrupt Qajar kings against the wishes of the Iranian population. These foreign powers did not take decisions made by the Iranian parliament seriously and often acted based on their own self-interests. For example, when the Iranian parliament announced Iran's neutrality during World War I, Russia and Britain ignored this national decision and sent forces into Iran.

REZA SHAH: THE FIRST PAHLAVI KING (1925–1941)

By the end of World War I, the Qajar dynasty that had ruled over Iran since the late eighteenth century was in disarray. It had failed economically and had lost support among Iranians. The time was ripe for a major change. In 1921, with the help of British officers, a self-made military man named Reza Khan orchestrated a coup that demolished the powers of the ruling Qajar king. After several years of consolidating his position as the country's strongman, Reza Khan crowned himself Reza Shah in 1925, the first king of the Pahlavi dynasty. (He chose Pahlavi, a pre-Islamic name, because it symbolically related him to the past glorious kings of Iran.)

Reza Shah's choice of regime was a constitutional monarchy over a republic, which many Iranian intellectuals wanted. Neighboring Turkey had just put an end to another despotic dynasty, the Ottomans, and replaced them with a republican regime. So it was natural for the people of Iran to want to replace its own despotic system with a republican one in which the people, rather than kings, would run the country. Iran was doomed, however, to have another king in Reza Shah.

In a hot national debate over the merits of a constitutional monarchy versus a republican system, many leading

After World War I, Iran's Qajar dynasty was in disarray. Economic instability made the time ripe for change. In 1925, with the help of British officers, an influential leader named Reza Khan crowned himself Reza Shah Pahlavi. He chose the pre-Islamic name Pahlavi to link himself to earlier great Iranian Kings.

clergy interestingly chose the monarchy. Reza Shah had made an agreement with the leading clerics that five Islamic jurists would be involved in government decision making to ensure that the government functioned within the Islamic context. He ignored the agreement, however, as soon as he took office.

THE MODERNIZATION PROCESS

Reza Shah was a strong nationalist who did whatever he thought necessary to lead Iran toward modernization. Like his counterpart Kemal Atatürk in Turkey, his ideal model for successful development was Europe. He considered Islamic traditions as impediments to Iran's path toward modernization. He was ignorant of the necessary criteria for effective development and was too stubborn to listen to those who understood the rationale for European success. Thus, his path to modernization was merely a blind imitation of the West, or the westernization of Iranian society. He failed to develop the country internally in a systematic way by building the essential physical and human foundations. Much needed to be done in the areas of education, economic independence, technological advancement, and especially social justice. He often forced his way on the Iranian parliament and Iranian people without any regard for human rights.

One should not overlook, however, some of the needed reforms orchestrated by Reza Shah. By secularizing the Iranian legal system, education, and bureaucracy, he curbed the influence of the clergy, who had dominated most aspects of Iranian society. He also centralized the Iranian administration system and created a disciplined army. He put down ethnic insurgencies and united the country. Among other improvements made during his rule were a modernized railroad system, the establishment of the University of Tehran, and allowing Iranian students to travel to Western countries for their college education. He also opened the National Bank of Iran, formed ministries of commerce and industry, and established a national census.

MODERNIZATION OR WESTERNIZATION?

Today Reza Shah is admired for preserving an Iranian sovereignty that was endangered by both internal and external threats. At the same time, his cruelty in dealing with the clergy and their traditional followers is cited as the primary reason for the direction taken by the Islamic Republic after its successful ascension to power in 1979. Impatient in his rush to secularize and westernize the country, Reza Shah banned the wearing of traditional Iranian and Islamic clothing in public. Women were told to cast off their traditional cover known as a *chador* and to wear Western dress. Men were ordered to wear Western suits, ties, and brimmed hats. Even the clergy were forced to shed their cloaks and turbans by which they were identified as clerics. The police enforced these rules, and violators were beaten and imprisoned.

In 1935, when some traditional followers of clerics in the holy city of Mashhad protested the imposition of these laws, Reza Shah ordered the bombing of a mosque inside which the protestors were gathered. In the eyes of the clergy and their followers, this was considered to be an ultimate act of disrespect for Islamic ideals. Reza Shah became an enemy of Islam.

During the early years of World War II, Iran declared its neutrality, and Reza Shah saw no need to participate in a European war. But as had happened during World War I, Western powers disregarded Iran's wish, and the country was occupied by Russian and British troops. In 1941, under external pressure, Reza Shah abdicated in favor of his young son and prince, Mohammad Reza, who became the second shah of the Pahlavi dynasty. Reza Shah was taken to Johannesburg, South Africa, where he died in exile.

MOHAMMAD REZA SHAH:
THE SECOND PAHLAVI KING (1941–1979)

Twenty-one-year-old Mohammad Reza Shah had neither his father's charisma nor his will to rule Iran. He was inexperienced and very much at the mercy of his foreign backers. At the same time, the Iranian parliament, under external pressure, changed its position and declared war against Germany. The Allies occupied and used Iran as a route to supply German-occupied Russia with food and war equipment. At the end of the war, when Hitler's forces were defeated, the Allies called Iran "the Victory Bridge."

Foreign forces remained in Iran from 1941 to 1946. The occupation fueled a nationalist fervor for independence from European powers. After the withdrawal of foreign forces, Iran searched for a way to rid itself of European political and economic dominance and their puppet Iranian kings. One of the first acts geared toward independence was the nationalization of Iranian oil by the Iranian prime minister, Mohammad Mosaddeq, in 1951. Mosaddeq's bold stand against British imperialism made him popular in Iran. He was helped by a group of religious leaders, including Ayatollah Kashani, who was also a member of parliament at the time—evidence again of religious figures becoming involved in Iranian politics.

THE MOSADDEQ CRISIS AND RETURN OF THE SHAH

British oil officials left Iran and issued a boycott against Iranian oil, a move that hurt Iran's economy. By 1953, the economy was suffering high unemployment and high inflation. The shah, under pressure from the Iranian people, left Iran and Mosaddeq officially became the country's leader. The British, however, convinced the United States to intervene and bring the shah back to power. By this time World War II had significantly weakened the British, and the United States had become a world power. Soon after the war ended in 1945, the United States and the former Soviet Union were competing for world political, strategic, and ideological domination in a rivalry known as the Cold War.

To protect American oil interests in the region on one hand and contain the Soviet Communist expansion on the other, the U.S. Central Intelligence Agency (CIA) became directly involved in Iranian internal affairs. The CIA, British intelligence, and Iranian officers supporting the shah orchestrated a coup that resulted in the overthrow of the government of Mosaddeq and reestablished the deposed shah's monarchy. To prevent further internal threats to the shah's government, the CIA provided training to the Iranian secret police, known as SAVAK (Sazmann-e Amniyat va Ittilaiat-e Keshvar), meaning the Agency for Security and Information (affairs) of the country.

SAVAK's job was to guarantee the regime's security and stability. In pursuing this assignment, the agency soon became notorious for its brutality and lack of respect for human rights. Many political opponents speaking in favor of democracy and human rights were falsely labeled as Communists, arrested, and often tortured or executed in prisons. American involvement in overthrowing Mosaddeq's government, and later its unconditional support for the controversial shah, gradually created a negative image of the U.S. government in the minds of Iranian intellectuals. America had become the shah's major ally and supporter in Iran.

Like his father, the shah is credited for modernization reforms. Iran's infrastructure, public health, and educational institutions were expanded. Highways, roads, bridges, railroads, water and sewage projects, factories, schools, as well as universities and hospitals were built. In the early 1960s, under pressure from the administration of U.S. president John F. Kennedy, the shah pioneered a series of reforms known as the "White Revolution," or the "Shah-People Revolution." The White Revolution

Mohammad Reza Pahlavi became the second king of the Pahlavi dynasty in 1941 after his father Reza Shah was pressured by British to abdicate from power. He continued the modernization process of Iran more aggressively during his 38 years reign. The 1979 Iranian Revolution forced Mohammad Reza Shah into exile and brought the Islamic Republic to power.

included projects such as land reforms, public ownership of industries, nationalization of forests, voting rights for women, workers' profit-sharing programs, and literacy and health corps educating and developing Iranian villages. These reforms, while looking good on paper, largely failed because of the rampant corruption of government agencies and officials. Some of these reforms, such as confiscating land from rich landowners and distributing it to peasants, and the emancipation of women, were opposed by certain religious leaders.

EXILING AYATOLLAH KHOMEINI

In 1963, Ayatollah Khomeini, a bold and popular Islamic religious leader, spoke out against the shah's White Revolution, prompting his followers to pour into the streets and denounce the ongoing reforms. Khomeini was arrested and then released. Soon after his release, Khomeini again was criticizing the shah's government for pushing legislation that granted U.S. military personnel immunity from local laws. The shah, like his father, was not in the habit of involving religious leaders in Iranian politics. Clerical influence had been significantly reduced, and those who dared to oppose his policies were labeled as fanatics and were punished. Khomeini was rearrested and sent to live in exile.

Since legal opposition parties were not tolerated, those who opposed the shah's government had to go underground and establish "guerrilla" (unofficial military) movements. During the 1970s, when the shah seemed to be secure in his position, there were many different guerrilla groups fighting the government. Their ideologies ranged from Communism to Islamic fundamentalism. Usually these opposition members, when identified and arrested, were labeled Communists. As such, most were persecuted and some were executed. By being labeled Communists, their elimination was supported by the U.S. government, which considered Communism to be a threat to American interests during the Cold War.

"WESTOXIFICATION" OF IRANIAN SOCIETY

During Richard Nixon's presidency, the shah and the U.S. government enjoyed a close relationship. Nixon, unlike Kennedy, was not critical of the shah's human-rights abuses. In the Nixon administration's "Twin Pillar" policy for the Middle East, Iran was considered the military pillar and Saudi Arabia the financial pillar. The shah fought for American interests in the Middle East and often publicly supported U.S. policies in the region. For example, throughout the Arab-Israeli wars, the shah supported Israel.

Iran also financially benefited from the misfortune of Arab countries. In 1973, when Arab countries protested America's support for Israel during the war and refused to sell their oil, Iran increased production. With the sharp drop in regional oil production, prices increased fourfold, providing Iran with a huge increase in revenue. Increased revenue, however, did not help the Iranian masses. The shah's ambition to put Iran among the world's economic and military giants led to massive government spending. This included the purchase of the latest military equipment, mainly from the United States. Huge government spending encouraged by Iran's overnight prosperity began to strain the country's inadequate infrastructure, overheat the economy, create high inflation, and cause shortages of consumer goods. One of the major problems was a steep increase in the price of real estate in Tehran. Many low- and middle-income people could not afford soaring rental costs. At the same time, the government was bringing laborers and professionals from abroad, offering them free housing and high salaries.

The government-run television stations were also promoting Western culture. Western soap operas, for example, were broadcast during prime-time hours. Many Muslim intellectuals found these programs distasteful for a traditional Muslim country. Many Iranians also believed the shah's government was destroying the traditional Islamic way of life and recasting the country in an American image. A popular Iranian author called the process "Westoxification," meaning that the society was losing its customs, values, and spiritual principles because it was becoming "intoxicated" by Western (interpreted as "materialistic") values. Universities became the bastions of opposition and were raided by SAVAK and police forces on a regular basis.

With society in disarray, some intellectuals returned to traditional Islamic values. By 1978, the opposition to the shah's regime had become widespread. Meanwhile, Khomeini had left his place of exile in Iraq and was living in France. From there, he communicated with his followers through smuggled cassette tapes and political pamphlets.

THE SHAH'S DEPARTURE

In 1978 students demonstrated in the holy city of Qum, located south of Tehran. Police put down the demonstration, resulting in six deaths. Throughout the country, more demonstrations followed, and many more demonstrators were killed. Those killed were considered martyrs by the demonstrators, who later became revolutionaries. Each fatality added more fuel to the fire of revolt, a flame that was burning out of control. Soon many unhappy Iranians were asking for the shah's removal from power. The shah had been put back in power by a 1953 coup orchestrated by the CIA and MI6, the British secret intelligent service. In the eyes of many Iranians, the shah was a tool of outside powers and an impediment in the way of Iranians' nationalistic and democratic aspirations.

To please the Iranian population, the shah, who was also suffering from cancer at the time, shuffled the membership of his cabinet, choosing individuals who were more popular with the masses. Although he appealed to the public with many promises, nothing seemed to work. Finally, on January 16, 1979, the shah and his family left Iran to live in exile. This was a sad occasion for a man who only several years earlier had crowned himself the successor of Cyrus the Great, the legendary king of Persia and founder of the first major Persian Empire, the Achaemenid, in a costly ceremony conducted before many official world dignitaries. Many could not believe how such a powerful man who had called himself the *Aryamehr* ("Light of Aryans") and had promised to turn Iran into a highly developed nation following the example of Japan, would leave his country and his people so soon after a political unrest.

The shah's departure paved the way for the arrival of Khomeini and establishment of the Islamic Republic of Iran. The Islamic Republic ended 2500 years of monarchy in Iran and started a new political era characterized by theocratic rule of the Shiite clerics.

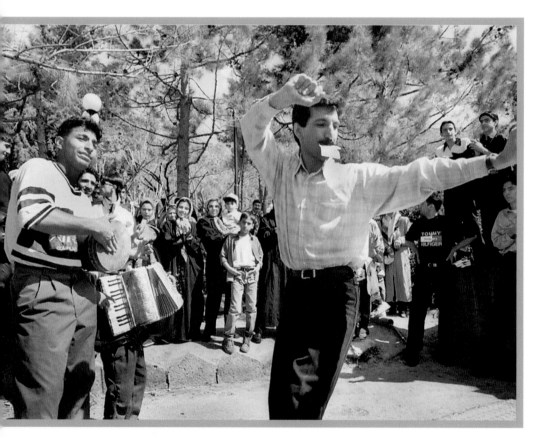

A man dances to celebrate the Persian New Year. Iran is home to many ethnic groups, each with their own dialect, customs, and traditions. Discrimination based on ethnicity is rare in Iran, and interethnic marriages are common.

5

People and Culture

With a current population of about 77 million, Iran is one of the largest countries in the Middle East. It is also one of the most diverse Middle Eastern countries in terms of culture and ethnicity.

POPULATION TRENDS

During recent decades, Iran's population has been one of the fastest growing in the region, having doubled since the Iranian Revolution in 1979. During the 1980s, there was a huge increase in the birthrate as a result of the new Islamic government's population policies (or, some suggest, the lack of policies). The new regime canceled the Family Planning Program that was put in place in 1967 to educate families about contraceptives and to improve the status of women in the areas of divorce laws and employment. Clerics considered the program to be a product of Western influence and ordered health officials to stop distribution of contraceptives. Ayatollah Khomeini advocated higher birthrates, calling unborn Iranian children the future soldiers of Islam. Policies such as offering material rewards for larger families encouraged a steep increase in population growth. Between 1980 and 1988, when Iran and Iraq were fighting a pointless and destructive war, the annual population growth rate reached well over 3 percent.

A DEMOGRAPHIC SUCCESS STORY

By the late 1980s, Iran was suffering from a number of social and economic problems. Cities were overcrowded and polluted, unemployment was high, there were not enough schools for the growing numbers of youths, and even paper and pencils were in short supply. The government began to reevaluate its population policies. In 1989, the national family planning program was revived. The government encouraged women to wait three to four years between pregnancies and for families to limit themselves to three children.

During the 1990s, the government began a bold campaign against population growth. The government-controlled news media began advertising the benefits of smaller families. Different institutions such as the Ministry of Education, Culture, and Higher Education and the Ministry of Health and Medical Education were asked to incorporate information on population, family planning, and mother and child health care in curriculum materials. Punitive measures such as restricting maternity leave benefits for mothers who have more than three children were implemented. Contraceptives and even sterilization became accessible from family planning clinics without cost to families. More than 15,000 of these mobile clinics were located throughout the country.

Unlike a decade earlier, clerics became actively involved in the national crusade for smaller families. They went so far as to encourage male and female sterilization along with other birth control means. The government even sponsored a condom factory in its attempt to make contraceptives more readily available. Perhaps the most effective policy was one that required couples to take a family planning class before receiving a marriage license. This was a somewhat innovative approach, since it required males as well as females to learn about contraception and family planning.

A combination of the foregoing factors, plus a dramatic increase in female literacy, caused a significant drop in population growth since 1990. By 2010, the natural rate of increase dropped to 1.25 percent, comparable to that of many developed countries. The birthrate was 18.5 per 1,000 and the death rate 5.9 per 1,000 people by 2010. Iran's total fertility rate—the average number of children born to a woman in her lifetime—also plummeted. In 1977, it was a whopping 6.6 (4.5 urban and 8.1 rural), but by 2010 had dropped to 1.9, somewhat below the replacement rate of 2.1. The extraordinary success of Iran in reducing its population growth in such a short period has made the country's population policy a significant model to be considered by other developing countries.

DISTRIBUTION OF POPULATION

Iran's population distribution has been greatly influenced by a rapid pace of rural-to-urban migration. This trend started in the 1960s and shows no sign of slowing down. Today, about 68 percent of Iranians live in cities, and rural areas are declining in population. One of the main reasons for this trend is a great gap in the standard of living that traditionally has existed between rural and urban areas. There has been considerable improvement in the lives of villagers, but city life, with its promise of entertainment, job opportunities, and excitement, sounds more attractive to rural youth than farming in remote villages. The fact that about 70 percent of the Iranian population is under 30 years of age increases the likelihood of movement to urban life.

Total Fertility Rate by Province, Iran, 2000.
Source: Iranian Ministry of Health and Medical Education, UNICEF, and UNFPA,
Demographic and Health Survey Iran 2000, Preliminary Draft Report (2002).

The Tehran metropolitan area remains the most attractive destination for immigrants from elsewhere in the country. More than 12 million people, or 1 of every 6 Iranians, live in Tehran Province. The average population density for the country is 121 per square mile (47 per square kilometer). In Tehran Province, however, the density is more than 11 times higher, about 1,500 people per square mile (579 per square kilometer). The agriculturally fertile provinces of Gilan and Mazanderan on the southern shores of the Caspian Sea are the next most crowded Iranian provinces. The city of Tehran, with a population of more than 8.5 million, is Iran's largest city and the world's twenty-first largest urban center. Other cities with a population of more than one million are Mashhad, Esfahan, Tabriz, Shiraz, and Karaj.

MANY DIFFERENT PEOPLES

Iran is one of the most ethnically diverse countries of the Middle East. Its location along the ancient Silk Route linking two major cultural hearths—China and the eastern Mediterranean—plus several thousand years of civilization, made it an attractive destination for immigrants. Throughout its long history, immigrants came both as invaders and as peaceful settlers. When they found themselves within the domain of Iranian culture, after a while they too adopted Iran as their home and contributed to further development of Iranian civilization.

Modern Iran is an ethnic and cultural mosaic. A visitor traveling within the country will see a variety of languages, customs, clothing, music, arts, and foods. Physically, Iranians are a diverse people, ranging from light-skinned populations along the Caspian coast to dark-skinned populations along the Persian Gulf. Ethnically, the dominant group is Persian— people who trace their roots to early Aryan immigrants who established the first important Iranian empires. Persians form about 50 percent of the current Iranian population and are the most widely distributed people throughout the country. For most of Iran's political history, Persians have ruled the country.

Other ethnic groups include Azaris, Gilakis, Mazandaranis, Kurds, Arabs, Lurs, Balochs, and Turkomans. There is no social prestige associated with any particular ethnic group. Also, prejudice and discrimination based on ethnic origin is rare in Iran. Interethnic marriages are common. Due to a long history of coexistence, most modern Iranians are of mixed ancestry and their ethnicity is difficult if not impossible to recognize based on physical appearance. Tehran is the most ethnically diverse Iranian city.

Some ethnic groups have not yet settled in cities and continue to live a nomadic lifestyle. Their number is estimated to be about 1.5 million, most of whom are pastoral nomads. Some of the nomads, such as Bakhtiaris, Kurds, Lurs, Gilakis, and Baluchis, are descendants of original Aryan nomads who entered the Iranian Plateau during the second millennium B.C. and still live on the slopes of the Elburz and Zagros mountains. Other groups such as the Qashqais, Turkomans, and Afshars are descendants of Mongols and Turks who came later. Classic films, such as *Grass* and *People of the Wind,* have documented the seasonal migrations of Bakhtiari nomads in western Iran.

LANGUAGES

Travelers driving on the roads between Iranian provinces are surprised by the variety of languages and dialects they can detect listening to their car radios. They can shift from one station reading Persian poetry to another one playing Turkish songs, and then change again to another station broadcasting in Kurdish. Iran is quite unusual among the world's nations in this respect. It is one of the few countries in which three linguistic families—Indo-European (Indo-Iranian), Altaic (Turkic), and Afro-Asiatic (Semitic)—are used by different groups, and occasionally even by the same people on different occasions!

Although numerous languages are spoken, the Indo-Iranian languages are the most widely used throughout the country. About two-thirds of the population speaks some type of Indo-Iranian language. The most important Indo-Iranian languages are Persian, Kurdish, Luri, Bakhtiari, Baluchi, Dari, Gilaki, Mazandarani, and Armenian. Persian is the official language of the country and the language of business and official communications. Different dialects of Kurdish are spoken among Iranian Kurds who live in western Iran, mainly in the provinces of Kurdistan and Kermanshah. Luri and Bakhtiari are spoken by Lurs and Bakhtiaris who live on the slopes of the Zagros Mountains. Baluchi is spoken in the eastern provinces of Sistan and Baluchistan, and Dari is spoken in parts of Khorasan, especially areas near the border of Afghanistan. Gilaki and Mazandarani are the local dialects of people who occupy the provinces of Gilan and Mazandaran on the northern slopes of the Elburz Mountains. Armenian is the language of Iranian Armenians who live in Tehran and in northwestern parts of Iran.

Farsi (or Parsi) is the official linguistic term for Persian. It was introduced by the early Aryan immigrants. The name of the language was changed from Parsi to Farsi in the seventh century A.D. when the Arabs ruled Iran. Since the Arabs could not pronounce the letter *P* (the sound does not exist in the Arabic alphabet), all the *P* sounds in Persian words were converted to *F*, a letter they could pronounce. Two centuries of Arab rule thus left its imprint on Iranian culture and Persian language. In addition to Parsi being called Farsi, the Persian language has been filled with Arabic terms that have been borrowed during many centuries of cultural contact.

Linguistic scholars recognize three forms of Persian: Old and Middle Persian, used in the distant past, and the Modern form. Modern Persian became dominant with the arrival of Arabs and Islam in the seventh century A.D. The alphabet was changed to Arabic with a number of additional characters to accommodate sounds that did not exist in the Arabic language. Although Modern Persian uses the Arabic alphabet, it is a totally different language than Arabic. Unlike Arabic, it does not have masculine and feminine words, and it is easier to learn than Arabic.

Modern Persian is spoken with many dialects. Each region has its own specific dialect and accent. For example, a person from Esfahan speaking his own dialect (known as Esfahani) is easily distinguished from a person from Mashhad who speaks in the Mashhadi dialect. The most commonly used dialect is the dialect of Tehran, the country's capital. Often the Tehrani dialogue is used in the media, including movies, national radio, and television.

Although Iran is the main Persian-speaking country, Persian is also spoken outside the current boundaries of Iran in parts of Afghanistan, Tajikistan, and by Iranians in southern Persian Gulf countries. An examination of Persian vocabulary can help us to understand its Indo-European roots. Some of the English words with Persian origin are: shawl, pajama, khaki, kiosk, divan, lilac, jasmine, julep, jackal, caravan, checkmate, and bazaar.

RELIGION AND CULTURE

As mentioned previously, during the seventh century A.D., the invading Arab-Islamic army brought the religion of Islam to Iran. Soon after its introduction, Islam became popular among Iranians, and many converted to the new religion and embraced its ideals.

SHIITE ISLAM

Iranians, however, did not accept the religion of their invaders in its imported form. From the beginning, there was a great interest in the Shiite sect of Islam in Iran. After the death of the Prophet Muhammad in 632, Islam was divided into the Sunni and Shiite branches. The difference between the two is not as much theological as it is political. Soon after the death of Muhammad, Muslims disagreed about the legitimacy of his successor. Most Muslims accepted the decision by the heads of powerful clans that Abu Bakr, Muhammad's close friend and father-in-law, should be the next leader. But another group of Muslims strongly believed that the succession should continue in the family line of Muhammad and therefore the next head should be his cousin and son-in-law, Ali. This group became known as the Shiite al-Ali, meaning the partisans of Ali. Through time, the word al-Ali was dropped from the end of the term.

Though today Shiites make up only about 15 percent of the world's nearly 1.6 billion Muslims, in Iran Shiism is the main belief system. In fact, Iran is home to the world's largest Shiite population. During the sixteenth century, the Safavid dynasty made Shiism Iran's official religion, and by the mid-seventeenth century the majority of Iranians were Shiite (Shias.) Gathering under the banner of Shiism, the country became united and was able to resist the expansionist tendencies of the emerging Turkish Ottoman Empire to the west. Shiite clerics, however, had never controlled the national government as they do now under the Islamic Republic of Iran.

FOUNDATIONS OF ISLAM

Muslims, like Christians and Jews, are monotheistic, believing in one God. The God of Islam is the same as the God of Abraham, Moses, and Jesus. God is called "Khoda" in Persian and "Allah" in Arabic. Although Muslims consider Islam a continuation of Judeo-Christianity, they do not accept the concept of the trinity. According to Muslims, Muhammad was chosen by God to be his last prophet in the line of Abraham, Moses, and Jesus. The Qur'an (Koran), the holy book of Islam, was revealed to the Prophet Muhammad through the Angel Gabriel. The Qur'an is believed to be the exact word of God, and today there is only one Arabic version of the holy book.

The Prophet Muhammad serves as the ideal model for every Muslim man. Muslims believe that human beings are responsible for their deeds and will be judged on Judgment Day. On that day, there will be a resurrection of body and soul so everybody can face trial. If people's good deeds prevail, the eternal heaven awaits them, and if their bad deeds prevail, they will be inhabitants of hell. According to Muslims, God

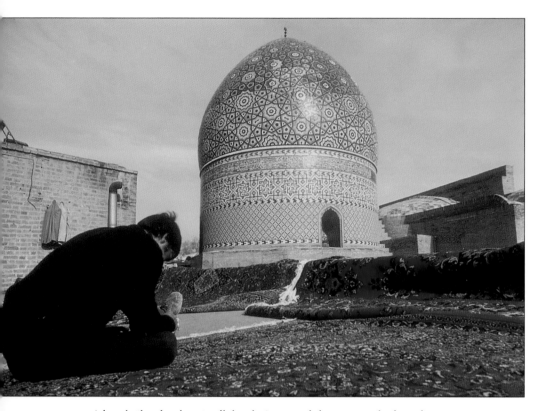

Islam is the dominant religion in Iran, and the country is dotted with shrines like this one. Shiite Muslims, although making up only 15 percent of the world's Islamic population, are the dominant sect in Iran.

is compassionate and merciful. They believe that he has sent prophets to lead them along a straight path and it is their religious duty to follow that path. The path of God is explained in the Qur'an and in the Hadith, books that document the Prophet Muhammad's sayings and deeds.

THE CONCEPT OF IMAMATE

A major Shiite belief that is not shared by Sunnis is the concept of imamate (the office of Imam, or Muslim religious leader).

According to Shiites, after Muhammad's death, 12 of his descendants served as political as well as spiritual leaders of the Muslim community; thus, Iranian Shiites are known as Twelver Shiites. Like the Prophet, these Shiite Imams were considered to be sinless and had the ability to interpret the inner mysteries of the Qur'an and the sharia (Islamic law).

According to Shiites, the imamate started with Ali, the Prophet Muhammad's cousin and son-in-law, and continued through his male offspring. According to Twelver Shiites, the Twelfth Imam never died. It is believed that he is spiritually among his followers and that he will someday return as Mahdi, or Messiah. Shiites' concept of Mahdi is similar to the concept of Jesus in Christianity. Mahdi, according to Twelver Shiites, is Lord of the Time, and devoted Shiites await his arrival; whenever his name is called, people rise as a sign of honoring his presence. His birthday is always a joyous occasion.

Iranian Muslims, like other Muslims throughout the world, believe in the Five Pillars of Islam. The first pillar is *Shahada*, or profession of faith that indicates oneness of God and Muhammad, God's last prophet. The second pillar is the ritualized daily prayers called *namaz* in Persian. The third pillar is *zakat*, or almsgiving, which should be used to take care of the needy and the necessities of the Islamic community. The fourth pillar is fasting (*roozeh* in Persian) during the holy month of Ramadan, the month in which the Qur'an was revealed to the Prophet Muhammad. The fifth pillar is *hajj*, a pilgrimage to the city of Mecca in today's Saudi Arabia, where the holiest construction in Islam, the Ka`ba, or house of God, is located.

RELIGIOUS MINORITIES

While Shiites make up 90 percent of the Iranian population, there are other religious groups living in Iran as well. About 9 percent are Sunni Muslims and 1 percent are Christians, Jews, Zoroastrians, and Bahais. Sunni Muslims are scattered around Iran, living mainly in border areas. Most Kurds, almost all Baluchis and Turkomans, and a small portion of Arabs are Sunni. Educated Shiites do not distinguish much between Shiites and Sunnis and consider Sunnis as fellow Muslims. Most Christians are Armenians and Assyrians, groups who were the original Iranian Christians. They are recognized as an official religious minority by the Islamic Republic and have their own representatives in Iranian parliament. There are also small numbers of Roman Catholics, Anglicans, and Protestants who were converted by Christian missionaries in Iran during the last two centuries.

Jewish history in Iran dates to the sixth century B.C. when Cyrus the Great released captive Jews. Many of today's Iranian Jews are descendents of those Jews who chose to remain in Iran. Like Christians, Jews are considered "people of the book" and are recognized as a legal religious minority by the current Iranian regime. They choose their own representatives to serve in the parliament. Currently, there are an estimated 30,000 to 40,000 Jews in Iran, most of whom live in Tehran. Jews do not enjoy the same prosperity that they had during the Pahlavi regimes. This has resulted in an out-migration of many Iranian Jews to Israel and the United States. Political hostility between the Iranian and Israeli governments has been a reason for occasional mistreatment of Jews by the Islamic government.

Today, there are still some 3,000 Zoroastrians in Iran, most of whom live in Tehran, Kerman, or Yazd. As members of an officially recognized religion, Zoroastrians have their own representatives in the Iranian parliament. There are also some 350,000 Bahais in the country. Bahaism is a faith that began in Iran during the 1840s as a reform movement within Shiite Islam. It is not recognized as an official religion, and Bahais have not been treated well by the country's Shiite clergy. Soon after the faith's emergence, Bahais were considered heretics of Islam and were persecuted. During the Pahlavi regimes,

Bahais were prosperous and free to proselytize (seek converts to) their faith. The current political regime has not allowed Bahais to proselytize, and many members of the faith have complained about being harassed by government officials.

In February 1979 thousands of Iranians came to witness the return of Ayatollah Ruhollah Khomeini to Iran after more than fourteen years of exile. Soon after his return, Khomeini built a coalition that established Iran as an Islamic Republic and himself as the Supreme Religious Leader of the country.

6

Government and Politics

While Iranians almost unanimously opposed the shah's government, they seemed uncertain about the kind of government they actually wanted. Most people wanted a government that was politically independent from outside powers. They did not want a government that would promote Western culture at the expense of Iranian and Islamic values. They wanted a government that was democratic and that respected human rights. People also hoped for leadership that could manage the national economy more efficiently and create jobs and access to opportunities regardless of people's socioeconomic class. Most of all, they wanted a government that was not corrupt. Did the next government satisfy these legitimate demands? This is a question that has not yet been fully answered.

RETURN OF AYATOLLAH KHOMEINI

As has been discussed, many opposition groups fought against the shah's regime. The best-organized of these groups, and those with greatest support of the Iranian masses, were the Islamic groups led by Khomeini. Four days after the shah's departure, Khomeini ended his 14-year exile abroad, and in January 1979, he entered Iran and received an unprecedented welcome from the Iranian people. With his great confidence and charisma, Khomeini appealed to Iranians from all different walks of life. Soon after his return, he put together a coalition of conservative clerics, secular leftists, nationalists, and moderate reformers, all of whom firmly believed in his sincerity and leadership skill.

Khomeini first had to confront the shah's appointed prime minister, who was still running the country. Before his departure, the shah had installed Shapur Bakhtiar, a popular senior politician, to this office. The armed forces remained loyal to Bakhtiar. Upon his arrival, Khomeini also appointed his own provisional prime minister, Mehdi Bazargan. Bazargan was a popular author and engineer with deep roots in the religious community. He also was an old colleague of Bakhtiar's from the National Front Party. Iran now had two different governments, one of which would have to step down.

Bakhtiar tried in vain to convince skeptics that his reformed secular government was a better choice for Iran than Khomeini's religious government. But demonstrators wanted power to be transferred to Khomeini and his appointee, Bazargan. They still considered Bakhtiar the shah's appointee; his survival would mean the continuation of a monarchy in Iran. The followers of Bakhtiar's regime were also greatly outnumbered by followers of Khomeini and Bazargan.

Some people worried that a military coup might save the shah's regime as it had in 1953 during Mosaddeq's era. This time, however, the wounds were too deep to cure and Iranians were too anxious for a new regime. When the Iranian armed forces declared their neutrality in conflicts between revolutionaries and the former regime, Bakhtiar had to step down from his post. Power was transferred to Khomeini and his revolutionaries.

THE ISLAMIC REPUBLIC

On April 1, 1979, a national referendum recognized the "Islamic Republic" as the legitimate government of Iran. The Islamic Republic, with its Islamic constitution, replaced the constitutional monarchy of the Pahlavi regimes. It is interesting to note that the Islamic Republic's constitution was mainly modeled after the French presidential parliamentary system. The key difference, however, was the insertion of a provision that granted the ultimate authority to a supreme religious leader, known as *vali-ye faqih*, meaning the ruling jurisprudent. The supreme spiritual leader, rather than the president or parliament, thus has the last word. Ayatollah Khomeini occupied this post until his death in 1989.

This revolution was unique because it ended some 2,500 years of on-and-off monarchy in Iran. Also, unlike many previous major political upheavals, such as the French Revolution or the Russian Revolution, which took so many lives, it was relatively bloodless. This revolution changed the path of Iran and Iranians both internally and externally. Today there are still debates concerning the need for revolution. Did it move the country forward on its path of modernization and development, or set it backward? Intellectuals both inside and outside the country are still debating questions such as these. What has become obvious is that the postrevolutionary Iranian government is far from being what so many Iranians hoped for and fought to gain. Many Iranians, however, still believe that the current government is a major improvement over that of the shah.

Iranians can now elect their leaders, at least theoretically. Due to a complicated system of filtering candidates on the basis of their ideological orientation, many qualified individuals are unable to run for government office. And even when they are elected by popular vote, they are powerless in the face of clerical domination of power. Hard-line clergymen playing partisan politics and trying to preserve the status quo often block reforms. Absolute power remains in the hands of the Supreme Leader and a powerful network of clerics and other influential individuals who are often not elected by Iranian people.

IRAN'S POLITICAL STRUCTURE

According to the constitution of the Islamic Republic of Iran, absolute sovereignty belongs to God and the Islamic government is the trustee of this sovereignty. Since clerics are the most qualified interpreters of God's words as revealed in the Qur'an and of the Prophet Muhammad's sayings and deeds collected in the books of the Hadith, they therefore should run the government. In addition, according to the constitution, an ayatollah (literally meaning the "Sign of God" on Earth), who has mastered the Islamic law, should serve as the country's supreme head. This clearly makes the government a theocracy. There are also other elements, however, within the system that are elements of a democracy (see figure on next page).

DEMOCRACY OR THEOCRACY?

Iran's political system is part democratic and part theocratic. The theocratic aspect often undermines the democratic processes, a fact that is the source of major complaint by contemporary Iranian reformists. Reformists seek changes in the system that will empower the president and parliament to implement their reformist policies. Although a majority of Iranians are Muslims who have great respect for the Islamic way of life, they do not appreciate the suffocating dominance of their country's affairs, including their private lives, by the clergy. They want more democracy and less theocracy in their government.

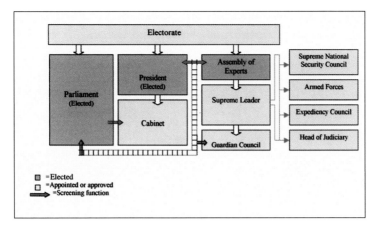

Political Structure of the Islamic Republic of Iran

THE SUPREME LEADER

What makes the system theocratic is the addition of two powerful positions—the office of the Supreme Leader and the Guardian Council. At the top of the Iranian power pyramid is the Supreme Leader. He is the commander of the armed forces, head of the judiciary system and national radio and television, and leader of the clergy in the Guardian Council. Some Iranians compare the role of the Supreme Leader with that of the shah, who could do whatever he pleased without being answerable to anyone. The Supreme Leader is selected for life, and not by the people but by his like-minded clerics. And he is not answerable to the Iranian population. Ayatollah Khomeini occupied this position until his death in 1989. Since then, Ayatollah Khamenei has occupied the position.

THE GUARDIAN COUNCIL

The Guardian Council is another theocratic office of the government. A very powerful body, the council's primary task is to ensure that bills passed by the parliament conform to Islamic principles. Bills do not become laws until approved by the council. Between 1988 and 1992, the Guardian Council rejected about 40 percent of all bills passed by the parliament.

The council is composed of 12 members, 6 of whom are theologians appointed by the Supreme Leader, and 6 who are jurists nominated by the judiciary system (which includes mainly clerics) and approved by the parliament. This council also has to approve the candidacy of individuals running for government offices and can veto candidates for presidency, parliament, local councils, and the Assembly of Experts (see following section).

These 12 nonelected members of the Guardian Council routinely block decisions made by some 200 elected officials in the Iranian parliament. This situation is what many Iranians recognize as being a deviation from the path of democracy. They also resent the fact that many highly popular individuals with excellent qualifications are unable to become candidates for office simply because their views are unacceptable to religious hard-liners.

ASSEMBLY OF EXPERTS

The Assembly of Experts is, at least in theory, the most powerful cog in the mechanism of Iranian politics. In practice, however, this is not what has occurred during recent years. The assembly consists of more than 90 clerics who supposedly appoint, oversee, and, if necessary, dismiss the Supreme Leader. The assembly recently has been criticized, however, for its passivity and submissiveness to the Supreme Leader. Members of the assembly are elected directly by the electorate and serve for eight years. This is a theocratic body, but members are elected democratically.

PARLIAMENT

The Iranian parliament, known as Majlis, is the most secular democratic body within the Iranian political structure. Begun in 1906, it also is the oldest democratic institution in the country. Members of parliament are elected by popular vote to four-year terms. Due to population increases since the 1979 revolution, the number of parliamentary seats has grown from 273 in 1980 to the current 290. Like Congress in the U.S. political system, people of different provinces elect their representatives to the parliament. Recognized religious minorities, such as Christians, Jews, and Zoroastrians, also elect their representatives. In the past, the parliament was occasionally forced to close due to pressure from the kings. Thus, the new Iranian constitution ensures that the parliament cannot be closed for any reason and elections will be held under any circumstances.

Among parliament's most important functions are drafting legislation, passing international treaties, approving state of emergency declarations and loans, discussing and approving the annual budget, and, if necessary, impeaching and possibly removing the president and cabinet ministers.

PARLIAMENT VERSUS THE GUARDIAN COUNCIL

Constant challenges by the Guardian Council pose the greatest problem for the parliament. Unlike members of parliament, who are often secular and reformists, most members of the council are conservative clerics. This difference often results in reformist bills being blocked by the conservative council. Supposedly, the council opposes bills that are in opposition to Islamic principles, but many of the bills they reject do not deviate from Islamic standards and ethics.

Due to this constant blocking of bills by the Guardian Council, a mediating office was established to serve as an intermediary between the parliament and the council. This Expediency Council faded away after Ayatollah Khomeini's death, but it emerged again during the late 1990s to attempt resolving conflicts between the parliament and the Guardian Council.

THE EXPEDIENCY COUNCIL

The Expediency Council consists of prominent religious, social, and political figures known for their ability to resolve conflicts. The council is a policy-making body with some legislative power. It also serves as an advisory body to the Supreme Leader.

THE PRESIDENT

Another elected office is that of president. Symbolically, at least, this office represents the most noticeable difference from the shah's regime. In the past, Iranians were not able to elect important individuals such as presidents. At the beginning of the revolution, this office was occupied by secular individuals such as Abolhassan Banisadr and Mohammad-Ali Rajai, but for the next six terms the office was occupied by cleric presidents, Ayatollah Ali Khamenei, Hojjatolislam Hashemi Rafsanjani, and Hojjatolislam Mohammad Khatami, when all three served for two consecutive terms. In 2005, however, the office was again returned to secular individuals when Mahmoud Ahmadinejad was declared the winner of the national presidential election. In a highly controversial and disputed presidential election, Ahmadinejad was reelected as president in 2009. The president heads the executive branch of government. His primary job is to ensure the rule of law by implementing the nation's constitution. He is in charge of the day-to-day running of the country. The president is elected for four years and can serve only two consecutive terms.

PRESIDENT VERSUS SUPREME LEADER

Khatami's landslide victory in 1997 was influenced by promises to end government corruption, reform the economy, implement the rule of law, respect the human rights of individuals, stop the harassment of intellectuals and free-thinking people by government thugs, empower women, and relax the harassment of youth by the morality police. When he took office, however, he had to face conservatives and their uncompromising views regarding reform and change. His proposed reforms were restricted by conservative clerics of the legislative and judiciary branches, and by the absolute authority of the Supreme Leader. It is the Supreme Leader, rather than the president, who controls the armed forces and has the last word. In Third World countries with rudimentary democratic processes, whoever controls the armed forces usually controls the country.

THE CABINET

After his election, the president selects his cabinet ministers, who must be approved by the parliament before they can begin their duties. Also, since clerics are wary of the potential westernization of Iranian society, they constantly monitor the activities of ministers dealing with cultural and social issues. The cabinet consists of some 20 ministers and is chaired by the president or by the vice president in his absence.

SUPREME NATIONAL SECURITY COUNCIL

The Supreme National Security Council coordinates foreign policy, defense, and security issues. Their decision-making meetings are chaired by the president and usually involve representatives of concerned ministries and institutions. Due to the importance of the council's decisions, its ministers report directly to the Supreme Leader.

ARMED FORCES

The Supreme Leader also heads the country's armed forces, of which there are two branches: the regular force, which retains almost the same structure as the prerevolutionary military, and the Islamic Revolutionary Guard Corps (IRGC), which is a postrevolutionary force. The IRGC was initially put together to protect the revolutionary leaders and guard against antirevolutionary threats. It was a counterbalance to the regular army, which was believed to be pro-monarchy.

In the beginning years of the revolution, the IRGC fought against rival groups such as the Islamic Marxist Mojahedin-e Khalq and the leftist Fedaiyan-e Khalq. It also put down ethnic

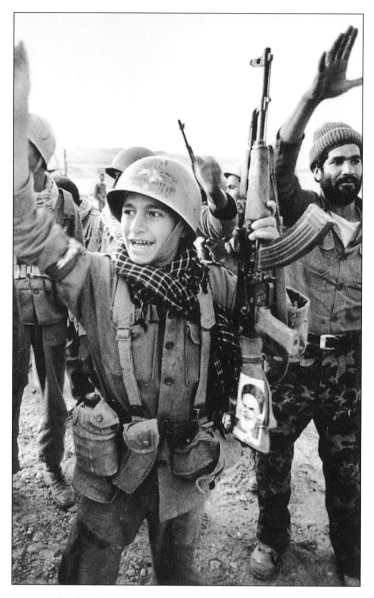

In 1980, shortly after the revolution that ousted Shah Mohammad
Reza, the neighboring nation of Iraq invaded Iran, hoping for an easy
victory. Iraqi leader Saddam Hussein incorrectly assumed that Iran
was too disorganized to defend itself, and a bloody conflict raged
for eight years, ending in a standoff.

insurgencies by separatist Kurds, Baluchis, and Turkomans. It was during the eight-year war with Iraq, however, that the IRGC matured and gradually developed its land, air, and sea divisions to become a full-fledged military force. The IRGC has the Basij, the most powerful paramilitary organization in Iran, under its wing. Today, it is believed to be the most powerful protector of Ayatollah Khomeini's revolutionary ideals and the strongest weapon in the hands of clergy.

MAJOR CRISES

Since its beginning, the Islamic Republic of Iran has faced many internal and external challenges. The most significant challenge came from the war with Iraq, a conflict that was both socially and economically disastrous for the nation. The second challenge came from the hostage crisis that antagonized the United States and impacted many of Iran's other foreign relations. The third crisis, however, was a homegrown one. Years of dissatisfaction with government's social, political, and economic policies resulted in bloody street demonstrations following the disputed victory of Ahmadinejad in the June 2009 presidential elections.

THE HOSTAGE CRISIS

On November 4, 1979, militant Muslim students, demanding that the U.S. government return the exiled shah—who had entered the country for medical treatment—to Iran, seized the American embassy in Tehran, taking 53 Americans hostage. The students said they would free the hostages when the shah was handed over to Iran to face justice. Diplomatic relations between Iran and the United States were immediately severed. Washington did not return the shah and retaliated by freezing more than $10 million in Iranian assets held in the United States. The United States also attempted a military rescue that failed, resulting in the loss of eight American military personnel.

After 444 days of confinement, the United States struck a deal with the Iranian government, and the hostages were released on the eve of President Ronald Reagan's inauguration. Many American political analysts believe that Jimmy Carter, who was running for reelection to the U.S. presidency, lost the election because of his handling of the hostage crisis.

THE IRAN-IRAQ WAR

On September 22, 1980, Iraqi forces invaded Iran in an attempt to annex the Shatt-al-Arab (Arvand Rud) estuary, whose centerline formed the southernmost portion of Iran's western border with Iraq. While there were long-standing regional rivalries between the two neighboring countries, the continuous conflict over the estuary was the main culprit for the invasion.

During early 1970s an ongoing Kurdish rebellious movement against Iraqi central government was supported by the Iranian government. The separatist rebels frequently ambushed the Iraqi army personnel using weapons supplied mainly by Iran and then retreated in Iranian territories to escape retaliation. By the mid-1970s the Iraqi government was frustrated. Its military power was much weaker than Iran's, which was equipped with advanced weapon systems purchased mainly from the United States. The Iraqi government was pressured by Iran's government to sign a border agreement regarding the river compromising the Iraqi ambition of controlling the whole estuary. In response the Iranian government stopped supporting the Iraqi Kurdish separatist movement, which if successful could have become problematic in Iran, which has a sizable Kurdish population. Soon after the agreement the Kurdish movement was brutally crushed by the Iraqi armed forces, and their main leader Mulla Mostafa Barezani fled to Iran.

By 1979, the year of the Iranian revolution, Saddam Hussein, who had been vice president during the 1975 border settlement with Iran, was the Iraqi president. For him the time was ripe for taking advantage of Iranian weakness, reversing the 1975 border settlement, making some territorial gains, and perhaps controlling the oil-rich Iranian province of Khuzestan, which had a large Arabic-speaking population. A war against Iran also could put an end to religious propaganda by Khomeini's government against neighboring Arab regimes, especially the regime of Saddam Hussein.

Hussein believed that Iran was too torn apart by revolution to defend itself against the revitalized Iraqi army. But that proved to be a serious miscalculation. Though during the beginning months of the war, the Iraqi military made some advances, within a year Iraqi forces were expelled from invaded territories and were on the defensive. The Iranian revolutionary guard forces, along with the regular army and the volunteer militia (basij), fought with revolutionary fervor and defeated the much better equipped Iraqi army. In 1982 when most Iraqi forces were out of Iran, however, Khomeini's government made a major mistake by rejecting the ceasefire along with a significant amount of compensation money offered by the Saudi government to cover the war damages. Iran continued the war on Iraqi soil, hoping to capture the Iraqi port of Basra inhabited mostly by a Shiite population, and eventually overthrowing Saddam's regime and replacing it with a friendly one.

The move was unsuccessful, however, and the bloody conflict dragged on for another six years. By August of 1988 when both sides were totally exhausted, with the help of the United Nations a ceasefire was finally reached. The war claimed an estimated one million lives, over one and half million wounded, and caused unbelievable hardship for millions of others on both sides. The economic cost of the war for Iran was estimated at more than $500 billion. By 1990 the Iraqi government dropped its claim of controlling the whole estuary and accepted the 1975 border agreement, which had established the centerline of the river as the official border of the two countries. That same year Iran and Iraq restored their diplomatic relations.

A group of Iranians prepare to burn pictures of President Bush and President-elect Obama just before Obama's inauguration in January 2009. The protesters were angry that the United States did not stop an Israeli airstrike of the Gaza Strip in December 2008 and a ground invasion in January 2009, which killed more than 1,000 Palestinians. The relationship between Iran and the United States has deteriorated since the Islamic Republic replaced the shah's pro-American government in 1979.

CHAPTER

7

U.S.–Iranian Relations

Relations between the United States and Iran remain antagonistic. Each side uses the other as a political scapegoat to encourage the passage of expensive defense budgets and to rally support for political actions. In addition, commercial relations between the two countries are very limited, mainly due to U.S. economic sanctions against Iran.

The U.S. government's grievances against Iran range from Iran's support for international terrorism, its hostility toward Israel, and to its attempts to acquire nuclear weapons and other weapons of mass destruction. Iran's grievances against the United States include America's support of Israel and its policies, its involvement in the affairs of Persian Gulf countries, the downing of an Iranian jetliner by American navy missiles in 1988 that killed 290 civilians, and the freezing of Iranian assets since the beginning of the Iranian

Revolution. The relationship between the two countries worsened especially following the terrorist attacks on the United States in September 2001. President George W. Bush included Iran on his list of "Axis of Evil" countries in his 2001 State of the Union address. Iran viewed this designation as evidence that the United States was unwilling to help improve relations between the two countries.

U.S. military forces occupy neighboring countries of Afghanistan and Iraq, and have military bases in other gulf countries such as Bahrain, Kuwait, and Qatar. It is little wonder that the Iranian regime feels both surrounded and threatened by the U.S. military presence. Adding to the sense of threat, the U.S. government has openly advocated regime change in Iran. It has funded opposition groups and supported secessionist ethnic minorities in Kurdistan and Baluchistan. The United States also has suggested that a military action is a possible option if Iran continues to pursue its uranium enrichment inside the country. While Iran denies that it is developing nuclear weapons, one can see why Iran might want to possess nuclear arsenals as deterrents against possible military threats from the United States and its allies in the region.

IRAN'S REGIONAL INFLUENCE

Iran is also trying hard to have friendly relations with the Muslim Middle East, hoping to neutralize attempts by the United States to isolate the country and form a united front against Iran. As Mohsen Milani notes in his article "Tehran's Take: Understanding Iran's U.S. Policy," the Iranian policy before and after the revolution has always been "U.S.-centric." Before the revolution, Mohammad Reza Shah regime's main foreign-policy goal was to please various U.S. governments, and it relied on the United States for the security of his regime and expanding his power in the region. The shah's regime accused and persecuted the domestic political dissidents as anti-Americans and as agents of Communism. This worked very well during the Cold War, when the main objective of the United States was containing the Soviet influence and spread of Communist ideology.

Since the revolution, different Iranian governments have also used the United States for promoting their domestic and foreign policies. The difference is that they have successfully used their anti-U.S. government attitudes and policies to consolidate their power inside the country and expand their influence in the region. Today, the Iranian political dissidents are labeled agents of the United States and England and are persecuted as enemies of the people and the revolution. This was particularly the case during the June 2009 presidential election crisis, during which many protestors were arrested or even killed by the government.

Different Iranian regimes have strongly opposed the Israeli occupation of Palestinian lands to gain popular standing with Arabs throughout the Middle East. Iran accuses the United States of failing to bring meaningful peace to the Israeli-Palestinian conflict. It also gains support from its condemnation of the continued Israeli occupation of most of the territories seized in the 1967 war from Arabs, and the Israeli invasion of Lebanon in 1982 and again in 2006. These and other accusations provide the Iranian regime with an opportunity to spread its sphere of influence throughout much of the Middle East. Such gains have been particularly strong in places such as Lebanon and Syria, and among Palestinian groups such as Hamas and Islamic Jihad in the Gaza Strip.

The 1982 invasion of Lebanon by Israel brought young Iranian revolutionaries to southern Lebanon to help their Shiite brothers and sisters, who were persecuted by both Israeli invaders and some Christian factional groups. Iran supported a militant group that became known as Hezbollah in southern Lebanon. This Iranian-backed group was responsible for attacking the U.S. Marine barracks and forcing the United States out of Lebanon in 1983. According to Hezbollah, rather than acting as peacekeepers, the American forces took sides in the country's ongoing civil war and supported certain Christian factions against Muslims.

During the last two decades, different Iranian regimes have provided Hezbollah with all types of support and helped them to develop militarily, economically, and socially. Ideologically speaking, Hezbollah has become a sort of political satellite for the Islamic Republic of Iran. Like the regime in Iran, Hezbollah is seriously concerned about Islamic solidarity, political sovereignty, and protection against Western influences. Leaders of Hezbollah frequently visit Iran and receive necessary advice in running their domestic and foreign affairs. The Islamic Republic's past and present figures are highly popular in southern Lebanon, and pictures of Ayatollah Khomeini and Ayatollah Khamenei are seen all over the region.

The friendship between the Islamic Republic and Hezbollah came to a test during the summer of 2006, when Israeli forces invaded and bombed Lebanon following the kidnapping of two Israeli soldiers by Hezbollah forces. During this war, which lasted for 33 days, Iran openly supported Hezbollah against Israel and its strong backer, the United States, without getting involved militarily. In the eyes of many Iranian politicians, the war between Israel and Hezbollah was in reality a proxy war between the United States and Iran. During the war, both Iran and the United States tested the military capability and political will of their allies. Hanging all over the major streets of Tehran were pictures of Hassan Nasrallah, the political and spiritual leader of Hezbollah. He was being viewed by young supporters of the Iranian Revolution almost like a rock star.

While brief in relative length, the war was brutal. It resulted in many civilian casualties, mainly from Lebanon, whose mutilated bodies were displayed frequently on state-run Iranian television. The fierce resistance put up by Hezbollah and the Israeli inability to crush Hezbollah forces provided both Hezbollah and the Iranian regime with a sense

During a demonstration to protest the results of the 2009 Iranian presidential election, riot police kick and beat a man in Tehran's Fatemi Square. The protestors were seeking reform.

of victory against Israeli forces and the United States. This is something that had never happened during earlier Israeli military campaigns against Arab neighbors. The uncertainty of Palestinian conditions under Israeli occupation has prompted the anti-American forces in the region to dwell on Palestinian-Israeli conflict to further their own geopolitical objectives. Any meaningful resolution to the conflict will significantly reduce the role played by countries such as Iran and Syria.

FAILED U.S. POLICIES?

During the past three decades, various U.S. administrations have sought to contain Iran. It is therefore ironic that American actions in the Middle East have worked totally against the policy of containment. Iran's two main enemies in the region, namely the Taliban and Saddam Hussein's regime, both have been eliminated by the United States, something that Iran was unable to accomplish alone. The elimination of these once formidable enemies has left Iran without major ideological and political rivals in the region. Further, it has provided Iran with opportunities to expand its influence in both Iraq and Afghanistan, particularly among the Shiite population of these countries. The inability of America and its allies to stop violence in Afghanistan and Iraq has contributed to a shattering of the U.S. image in the region. Iran has taken advantage of the situation and increased its role in these two countries.

IRAN AND UNITED STATES
SHARED INTERESTS IN AFGHANISTAN

A case in which the United States and Iran cooperated with the same goal in mind was Afghanistan. After years of bloody fighting among various political factions, by 1996, the Taliban finally managed to rule most of Afghanistan. The only group that managed to withstand the Taliban was the Northern Alliance, which was supported by Iran. During 1990, U.S. allies Pakistan and Saudi Arabia were supporting the Taliban, who worked closely with al Qaeda. Iran, however, cultivated a friendship with the Tajic ethnic group that speaks a language very close to Iranian Persian. The Tajic formed a resistant front against the Taliban, which became known as the Northern Alliance. This was also the force that cooperated with the invading U.S. troops in 2001 to liberate Afghanistan from the yoke of the Taliban. The United States and Iran worked together and exchanged vital intelligence to succeed in defeating the Taliban. One of the main grievances that Iran had against the Taliban was their exclusivist interpretation of Islam. The Taliban regard the Shiites as heretics. This belief led to a cruel massacre of Shiite Hazara (Hazareh) ethnic group in central Afghanistan at the hands of Taliban extremists.

A stable Afghanistan free of Taliban and al Qaeda is beneficial to both Iran and the United States. Both countries want to stop cultivation of opium and drug trafficking. They also want to defeat the Taliban and al Qaeda forces and rebuild Afghanistan. Iran has invested heavily in the reconstruction of Afghanistan, especially the western part of the country around the city of Herat. The economic prosperity and relative security have kept the forces of Taliban and al Qaeda out of this region. To improve the economy and social conditions of Afghanistan, Iran has pledged millions of dollars in aid and has helped in funding developing projects for infrastructure, education, agriculture, power generation, and telecommunications. Most of the trade products for western Afghanistan also come from Iran, which shares a long border with the country. Markets in cities like Herat are loaded with Iranian goods.

One thing, however, that Iran does not want to see is the permanent U.S. military bases in Afghanistan. Iran considers it a threat to its security and is hoping for total U.S. withdrawal after normalization of conditions in Afghanistan. To compete for power in Afghanistan and be able to retaliate any possible military threats from the United States, Iran has developed close ties with the Northern Alliance and some other warlords, insurgents, and anti-American forces inside Afghanistan.

SHARED INTERESTS IN IRAQ

Iran and the United States also share a number of common interests in Iraq. Both want Iraq to be a stable country with a strong economy. In 1982, two years after Saddam Hussein's army invaded southern Iran, Iranian forces drove out the Iraqis. At the time, however, Ayatollah Khomeini and some of his generals refused the cease-fire and war damages offered by the Saudi government. Instead, they decided to pursue the war inside Iraq, topple the regime of Saddam Hussein, and replace it with a friendly Shiite regime. To accomplish this, Iran fought six more years of war. In 1988, the two countries finally came

An Afghan Northern Alliance fighter cheers the U.S. striking of a Taliban position in 2001. Stability in Afghanistan is one of the common interests of Iran and the United States.

to their senses and signed a cease-fire, without any clear winner. Iran did not accomplish its goal of overthrowing Saddam's regime. Therefore, the Iranians were very pleased when the United States and its allies finally toppled the regime of Saddam Hussein.

The United States and Iran also do not want to see a politically divided Iraq. Iran does not want to see Kurds in the north, Sunnis in the center, and Shiites in the south divide Iraq into three separate countries. A new Shiite country independent of Sunnis and Kurds might offer an attractive choice and possibly a political satellite for Iran. But balkanization (breaking a country up along ethnic lines) would establish a precedent that ethnically diverse neighboring countries like Iran and Turkey cannot afford. Both Iran and Turkey have large Kurdish populations living within their territories. An independent Kurdistan in northern Iraq would encourage those Kurds inside these two courtiers to secede as well. This is something that Iran, Turkey, and Turkey's ally, the United States, do not wish to happen.

Although the United States and Iran share common interests in Iraq, they are also competing for power in Iraq as well as in the rest of the Middle East. At the beginning of the U.S. campaign against Iraq in 2003, the Iranian government was particularly nervous about the consequences of a clear U.S. victory in Iraq. Iran was under the impression that the U.S. military would not stop with Iraq after toppling the Iraqi regime. Iranians feared the next move would be to topple the other two unfriendly regimes in the region, namely Iran and Syria. As with Afghanistan, Iran hopes to see the total departure of U.S. military forces from Iraq, forces that Iran regards as threat to its national security.

Because of their common interests in the region, Iran and the United States need to establish a better relationship. Despite the anti-American propaganda by the Iranian government, the United State remains popular among many Iranians. America also is the major destination for Iranians who wish to leave Iran for a more free and prosperous foreign country. Today's Iranian youth look up to America as a source of technological, scientific, artistic, and democratic innovations and inspiration. Many Iranian families have relatives who live in the United States and are in constant contact with them. Although there is no clear demographic information about the number of Iranians in the United States, there is a common belief among Iranian Americans that there are at least one million Iranians living in the country. By and large, these Iranians are among the most highly educated and professionally successful U.S. minorities. They can act as a bridge that connects the two nations.

In the past, various Iranian governments have attempted to extend a hand of friendship to the United States. In most cases, however, these gestures have been ignored by the U.S. government. Former president Khatami, for example, traveled to the United States. In his various interviews, he made it clear that he wanted better relations between Iran and America. Instead of continuing the old trend of antagonism, he asked for improved communications that would help both countries better understand each other. Following the September 11 tragedy, Iranian president Khatami and the Supreme Leader Khamenei both condemned the terrorist act against innocent citizens. Many Iranians also showed their sympathies with the victims of the tragedy with candlelit vigils in streets of Tehran.

RELATIONS WITH OTHER COUNTRIES

Since the end of Iran's long war with Iraq, relations between the two countries have improved. Currently, for example, Iranian pilgrims are now allowed to visit the holy Shiite cities in southern Iraq, and the two countries have exchanged prisoners of war. Also, since the end of the Taliban regime in Afghanistan, Iran has had a good relationship with that country. Relations with gulf countries have improved significantly during Khatami's presidency. Although Iran and the United Arab Emirates have had disputes about some of the smaller Persian Gulf islands, their relations seem to be good.

Iran also has maintained friendly relations with Russia, which has been helping Iran with its economic development and supplying it with military equipment. Russia has also been involved in building a nuclear reactor in the southern Iranian city of Bushehr. The Chinese have helped Iran build major industrial plants and transportation facilities. Iran's relations with Japan and some western European countries also have been mutually beneficial.

The breakdown of the former Soviet Union resulted in the emergence of many new Muslim-dominated countries. This has greatly expanded Iranian influence within the region. Due to religious and historical ties with these lands and peoples, Iran has been able to expand its economic, political, and cultural influence and establish itself as a regional power.

Inaugurated in 2007, the Borzouyeh petrochemical complex in the industrial city of Assalouyeh to the south of Iran produces 1.28 million tons (1.2 million metric tons) per year of aromatic products including par-xylene and ortho-xylene, which is used in production of polyesters, synthetic fibers, pharmaceuticals, pesticides, paints, and phenol.

8

Iran's Economy

In 2009, Iran's gross domestic product (GDP)-purchasing power parity (PPP) was estimated to be about $827 billion. This places Iran in the nineteenth position among the world's economies and second behind Turkey in the Middle Eastern region. On an individual basis, however, Iranians do not fare as well. With some 77 million people, the per capita GDP-PPP is about $12,500, which ranks one-hundredth among nations. In 2009, Iran had approximately $81 billion in foreign reserves and gold. Only 21 other countries held greater financial reserves. In 2009, agriculture (10.9 percent), services (43.9 percent), and industry (45.2 percent), respectively, accounted for Iran's GDP.

AN ECONOMY IN TRANSITION

The Iranian economy can be classified as "transitional" because of ongoing changes in its structure. It is changing gradually from an economy centrally planned and government run to one based upon a free market, more like what we see in Western countries. The transition, however, has not been smooth and is not complete. Most of the economy remains under government ownership and control. The government owns and administrates the majority of heavy industry (i.e. steel, petrochemicals, copper, automobiles, and machine tools), major minerals, dams and large-scale irrigation networks, and power generation. It also maintains a tight grip on foreign trade, banking, insurance, radio and television, post, telegraph and telephone services, aviation, shipping, roads, and railroads. The small private sector is involved in most light industry, agricultural activities, animal husbandry, construction, some commerce, and many personal services. In addition to state and private sectors, there are many conglomerates known as *bonyads*, or religious or ideologically-based foundations. They are involved in most profitable international trades and transactions, some production, and distribution of goods throughout the country. The bonyads employ millions of Iranians and can be considered as the cooperative sector of the Iranian economy.

To become closer to a market economy, the Iranian economy needs more liberalization, which requires free-market pricing and lowering unnecessary trade barriers. It also needs more stabilization to bring often rampant inflation under control. According to Central Bank of Iran, inflation was brought down to 11.5 percent by February 2010. Private estimates, however, place it at more than 20 percent. The price of goods seems to increase regularly, and most Iranians constantly complain about the high cost of living.

The economy is also poorly taxed, highly subsidized, and heavily reliant on income from oil exports, which account for the bulk of foreign exchange. Petroleum earnings account for 60 to 70 percent of the government's budget. Taxes account for only a small portion of the country's government revenue, because much of the economy is tax exempt. Some activities are taxed, yet widespread tax evasion and bribing government officials to avoid payment are common practices. Subsidies on food, energy, and some other goods, government price controls, and rigid trade rules have hurt the economy. So have rampant corruption and the common practice of nepotism (hiring family members). Combined, these conditions have undermined the private sector, discouraged foreign investment in Iran, and severely hurt the economy.

Because the economy is weak, unemployment is high. In early 2010, the government estimated that 12 percent of the labor force was unemployed. Private sources, however, suggest that the number is at least twice as high. One of the main reasons for the high unemployment rate is the government's pro-natal policies during the 1980s. During the war with Iraq, government officials actively promoted higher birthrates and larger families. This led to an explosive birthrate and huge numbers of people who now seek employment. Today, about two-thirds of Iran's population is under 30. There are other problems. Many Iranians lack the skills needed in professional jobs. Also, tough labor laws discourage many employers from offering employees long-term contracts.

One of the positive aspects of Iran's economy has been its steady growth during the past two decades. Between 1991 and 2002, the economy grew at an annual average rate of about 3.4 percent. From 2002 to 2007, growth was about 5 percent per year. By 2010, it had slowed to around 1.5 percent. Unlike many Third World countries, extreme poverty (defined by the United Nations as below $1 per day) is not a problem in Iran. Although there are those who live below the poverty line (defined by the United Nations as below $2 per day), the biggest challenge for the government is a better redistribution of wealth and finding employment for a growing young population.

A BRIEF HISTORY OF IRAN'S ECONOMY

Before oil was discovered, Iran's traditional source of liveli-hood was agriculture. Most people farmed or raised livestock, although some also earned income through trade, services, and craftsmanship. Primary exports included quality handi-crafts, particularly textiles and carpets, as well as decorative gold, silver, copper, and brass items. But with the discovery of oil in 1908, petroleum gradually became the backbone of the country's economy.

With the emergence of the Pahlavi dynasty in 1925, the economy began to change again. Iran began to look toward European countries for models of development. Reza Shah attempted to modernize the country by stabilizing the cen-tral government, building an educational system, improving communications, and constructing roads and railways. The process of industrialization also began, though the emphasis was more on capital-intensive (machine-driven), rather than labor-intensive, industries.

The process of modernization continued more aggressively under Mohammad Reza Shah after he replaced his father in 1941. By then, the income from oil had increased and Iran had more educated professionals who could lead the nation to a more prosperous future. This shah's regime significantly expanded the country's physical infrastructure by building more roads, railroads, ports, airports, and industries, and by improving communications and services for urban areas. Until 1978, the economy was doing very well. The annual growth rate between 1960 and 1977 was around 10 percent—outstanding for a developing country.

Financial prosperity, however, was not reaching the needy people, and only a small percentage of the population ben-efited. Also, the shah's immense appetite for militarization diverted the country's modernization focus. A huge amount of money was spent on weapons. The shah's government failed to improve human conditions. He did not make the political system more democratic or improve the economic system by reducing the strong grip of economic monopolies. Neither did he reduce governmental corruption or develop programs to help the poor and dispossessed. His failure in these areas was a primary factor contributing to the 1979 mass uprising that brought the Islamic Republic to power.

ISLAMIZATION OF THE ECONOMY

The 1979 revolution that brought the clerics to power seriously disrupted Iran's development and economic growth. The per capita gross domestic product fell from about $8,000 in the late 1970s before the revolution to about $4,000 at the end of the war with Iraq in 1988. War, collapse of oil revenues, and economic mismanagement combined to cause a sharp drop in the country's economy. The revolutionary government had no real economic plan. It simply wanted to reverse many of the former regime's ongoing policies. The government began to take control of major industries from their private managers and confiscate many enterprises owned by the shah's sympathizers. The revolutionaries' main goal was to change the nature of the development plans from what they called "Westernized" to what they considered to be "Islamized." They "Islamized" Iranian banks by making them nonprofit organizations and giving interest-free loans (making money by collecting interest is forbidden in Islamic law).

In the name of confronting westernization, the government stopped the import of luxury goods from Western countries and cut funding for many existing development and construction projects. Iran, according to revolutionaries, needed to become self-reliant and independent from superpower intervention.

IDEOLOGY VERSUS EFFICIENCY

Under Islamic control, the revolutionary conglomerates known as bonyads (foundations) were given a free hand by the government. They rapidly monopolized Iran's main economic

enterprises. Bonyads believed that individuals with a revolutionary Islamic ideology were better suited to manage the country's
main institutions than were secular professionals. So it was "ideology," rather than "efficiency" and know-how, that became the
main qualifier for employment. In the name of ideology, a large
number of well-educated professionals were fired from universities, courts, and other institutions and were replaced by ideo-
logues known as "insiders" by revolutionaries. This approach led
to a serious brain drain through the emigration of a huge number of skilled professionals, managers, and entrepreneurs from
the country. Today, more than 3 million Iranians live abroad;
many of those left following the revolution.

IMPEDING EXTERNAL FACTORS
There also were external forces that had a negative impact on
the Iranian economy during the first decade following the
revolution. These factors included the Iran-Iraq War, a drop
in the price of oil, Western economic sanctions against the
country, and the freezing of billions of dollars of Iranian assets
abroad. War with Iraq was the most damaging factor. Nearly all
of Iran's oil income went directly to cover war expenses. The
preoccupation with war also set back the process of industrialization and other forms of economic development.

POSTREVOLUTIONARY ECONOMY
By the late 1980s, when Iran had already reached a cease-
fire agreement with Iraq and the revolutionary fever had
cooled down somewhat, the government began to realize its
past mistakes and looked for a new approach to economic
development. By the early 1990s, the government started to
privatize some small industries and invite both Iranians living abroad and non-Iranian investors to conduct business in
Iran. But there were also many problems that discouraged
such investments. Iranian business laws were easily subject to
abuse and manipulation. Corruption was widespread within

government and the bonyads. Government conservatism discouraged many potential investors, as did the country's gross mismanagement of matters pertaining to both politics and economics. Fortunately, during the 1990s, the economy began to grow, and its performance significantly improved during the following decade.

Most observers now believe that the economy stagnated because of the country's revolutionary political structure that placed power in the hands of those who directly benefited from chaotic economic and political conditions. The 1997 election of Mohammad Khatami as Iranian president was interpreted by some as a possible chance to liberalize the country's political and economic establishments. Khatami called for a total restructuring of the Iranian economy during the country's five-year plan (between 2000 and 2005). He announced a grand program to privatize several major industries, such as communications, postal service, railways, and petrochemicals. The five-year plan also sought to create 750,000 new jobs each year and to achieve an average annual increase in the gross domestic product (GDP) of 6 percent.

The plan attempted to reduce subsidies for basic commodities (including bread, rice, sugar, vegetable oil, wheat, and fuels) and introduce a range of fiscal and structural reforms. The plan, however, was not approved by the parliament during Khatami's presidency. Rather, it fell to incoming president Ahmadinejad and the conservative parliament to make it work. The country's GDP grew during Khatami's tenure mainly because of an increase in the price of oil. By 2005, the end of Khatami's second term, annual oil revenues reached about $48 billion compared to $13 billion in 1998.

THE ECONOMY UNDER AHMADINEJAD

Ahmadinejad came to power with a promise of changing the economy. His main campaign promises were to work for more equitable distribution of wealth, taking care of the poor, and ending the overwhelming corruption occurring at all levels of government. During his campaign, he traveled to remote areas of Iran, including some rural areas where no politicians had ever been. He vowed to become the champion of downtrodden people if elected. His slogan, which struck a receptive chord with the poor, was the promise to "take oil money to people's dinner table."

To reform the economy, Ahmadinejad dismantled the country's management and planning organization. This group had functioned for a half century and had been responsible for the management and investment of national wealth, especially oil revenues. Being a conservative politician, he worked closely with the conservative parliament members (who became the majority in the parliament by 2004) to pass the Khatami-initiated plan that called for privatization, antitrust legislation, and labor market reform. The plan was approved as the Fourth Development Plan (2005–2009). It also called for reforming education to better prepare and qualify the college graduates for successful integration into the global economy. Perhaps the most difficult task of the plan was reforming the unpopular labor laws that affected many workers who had supported Ahmadinejad's presidency. The plan also aimed to make life easier for business owners and employers who were held responsible for workers' health and income security. Under the plan, the burden of income security was transferred from employers to a public system of social security.

The government of Ahmadinejad is characterized by dominance of Iranian neoconservatives, a group known as the "New Rights." These neoconservatives were unhappy with the status quo during the presidency of Khatami. Of major concern was the Reform Movement that called for improved relations with the West, especially with the United States. The New Rights believed that the noble ideas of the 1979 Islamic Revolution had been gradually eroded during the 16 years of Khatami and Rafsanjani's presidencies. Therefore, they called

The weaving of fine handmade carpets is a traditional pursuit in many areas. Artisans in the city of Esfahan produce carpets as well as brass and copper household items.

for a return to the "roots of the revolution." They were nostalgic for the pristine decade of 1980s under their spiritual mentor Ayatollah Khomeini and for the turbulent years of the Iran-Iraq War, when they believed there was a true feeling of solidarity and comradeship among revolutionaries and a strong sense of national cohesion brought about by the 1979 Islamic Revolution. They wished to challenge the Western version of democracy in Iran with all its westernized signs, which in their minds were threatening the Islamic roots of the country.

The New Rights wanted to replace the Western ways of development and living with Islamic ideals. They called themselves the "Alliance of the Developers of Islamic Iran" and promised their followers a new order of prosperity and equality. They believed, unlike what reformists had sought, that there was no need to liberalize Iran's political system, and they rejected political reforms called for by the reformists that would reduce the power of the clergy, especially that of the Guardian Council. They believed the country needed economic development that would reduce Iran's dependence on the West and better distribute wealth among both urban and rural populations. With all its promises, Ahmadinejad's government has not delivered prosperity and equality and has not significantly improved the lot of Iran's poor and middle class.

Implementation of the fourth round of sanctions approved by the United Nations Security Council on June 9, 2010, is expected to further worsen the Iranian economy. The sanctions are imposed to deter the ongoing Iranian nuclear program, which the United States and its allies believe is for developing nuclear weapons. Iran, however, insists that its nuclear program is for energy development and other peaceful purposes. The main aim of sanctions is to stop or disrupt Iran's military purchases. The sanctions also seek to limit the power of the Islamic Revolutionary Guards Corps, which controls most of the national economy and is in charge of the country's nuclear program. These sanctions are expected to make foreign investments in Iran even more difficult than they are today.

POPULATION GROWTH, POVERTY, AND UNEMPLOYMENT

Rapid population growth, particularly during the 1980s, directly hindered economic growth and development in Iran. At the time of the 1979 Islamic Revolution, 36 million people lived in the country. By 2010, this number had increased to more than 77 million, many of whom were under 30 years of age. By 2010, the median age for Iran was reported at about 27 years, meaning less than half of the population is 27 or older. This young and demanding population has placed tremendous pressure on Iran's economy, services, and resources. Job prospects are limited and unemployment is high, about 13 percent in 2010.

WEALTH DISTRIBUTION

Many Iranians complain that a major goal of the 1979 Islamic Revolution—to achieve a more equitable distribution of wealth—has not been achieved. A 2002 report by Iran's Plan and Budget Organization disclosed that the wealthiest 20 percent of the population held 50 percent of the gross national product (GNP) and the 40 percent at the bottom of the income pyramid held only 16 percent of GNP. By 2005, the last year for which these data are available, the richest 10 percent of the population held nearly 30 percent of the country's wealth and the poorest 10 percent held only 2.6 percent.

GOVERNMENT'S ACCOMPLISHMENTS

On the positive side, the government has succeeded in reducing the country's previously soaring birthrate and in improving health conditions. Mortality rates are now significantly lower than during prerevolutionary times. For example, the infant mortality rate (number of children per 1,000 dying before reaching one year of age) has fallen from 104 in the 1970s to 43 in 2010.

Life expectancy has increased from 55 to 70 years during the same period. Today, access to health facilities is easily available to most Iranians, and the government has kept the cost of medicine and medical treatments low. There are also many colleges and universities, and the literacy rate has grown significantly for both men and women. Today, nearly 80 percent of the people over age 15 can read and write.

OIL-DEPENDENT ECONOMY

Iran's economy is highly dependent on the country's vast oil reserves and production. Oil production is government controlled, and most government spending is financed by the income from oil. Without oil revenues, Iran's economy would collapse. This dependency has made the economy very fragile, since changes in the price of oil can directly impact the country's five-year development plans. For example, in 1998, when the oil price fell below $10 a barrel, the country's economy was on the verge of collapse. Fortunately, the oil price rebounded and the economy was able to stabilize, including its ability to pay foreign debts. When a country relies on a single commodity as its primary source of livelihood, it is very much at the mercy of buyers. If buyers boycott the commodity, then the economy will collapse under pressure. The 1953 international boycott of Iranian oil weakened the Mosaddeq government, allowing it to be easily overthrown. Today, Iranian economists seek economic diversification, which they believe is essential for the country's future well-being.

OIL AND OTHER RESOURCES AND INDUSTRIES

Iran sits upon two of the world's most productive oil fields, those of the Caspian Depression to the north and the Persian Gulf to the south. The country's oil reserves, according to *Oil and Gas Journal*, are estimated to be 137.6 billion barrels, or roughly 10 percent of world's total. Iran is the second-largest producer of oil among the Organization of Petroleum Exporting Countries (OPEC), following Saudi Arabia. In 2008, Iran's daily production of oil was 4.2 million barrels, of which 2.4 million barrels per day were exported. The rest was used domestically. Iran is the world's fourth-largest exporter of oil, with most of it going to Japan, China, India, South Korea, and Italy, in that order. Most of Iran's crude oil reserves are located in giant onshore fields along a northwest–southeast belt running parallel to the Zagros Mountains. Khuzestan province is particularly known for its oil production. Among the most active fields are Ahwaz-Bangestan, Marun, Gachsaran, Agha Jari, and Bibi Hakimeh. Overall, Iran contains 40 producing fields, with 27 being onshore and 13 offshore. The government is currently working on improving and expanding offshore production.

Although Iran possesses vast petroleum reserves, it lacks adequate refining facilities. Therefore, it must import gasoline for its rapidly growing domestic needs. Iran's total refining capacity in 2009 was about 1.5 billion barrels a day, which is below its domestic consumption. The need for imported gasoline has become an economic problem for the country. During 2010, the United States and Israel were hoping to impose sanctions against Iran that included banning gasoline export to the country. Iran has, however, completed some foreign deals with China and a few other Asian countries to improve its refining capacity in the hope of becoming self-sufficient in gasoline production. The plan is to improve the country's refining capacity to 3 million barrels per day by expanding the existing refineries and building new ones.

NATURAL GAS

Iran ranks second behind Russia in proven reserves of natural gas. The country's deposits are estimated to be more than one trillion cubic feet (tcf), or about 15 percent of the world's total reserves. Most gas fields are located in the same areas as the oil deposits. Unlike the oil fields, however, most of the gas fields have not yet been developed. Iran hopes to increase production and become a major exporter of natural gas. Due to high domestic consumption, Iran has to import natural gas from other countries. For example, in 2008 Iran produced 4.1 tcf and consumed 4.2 tcf, with the shortage made up with natural gas imported from Turkmenistan. Around half of Iran's current total energy consumption comes from natural gas. Domestic consumption of this clean-burning fuel is expected to increase by 7 percent annually during the next decade.

NON-OIL RESOURCES

Other Iranian resources include iron, copper, zinc, lead, chromite, and manganese. There also are abundant reserves of such building materials as limestone, marble, clay, and construction rock. Other materials of use include glass sand, salt, kaolin, turquoise, coal, and sulfur. A recent use of satellite imagery helped in the discovery of a highly mineralized volcanic belt near the tectonic plate boundary along the inner Zagros range, roughly paralleling the railroad linking the cities of Qom and Kerman. This belt includes iron, chrome, lead, zinc, bauxite, manganese, coal, barite, and a massive amount of copper. Copper, with deposits estimated to be 2.6 billion tons (2.4 billion metric tons), is Iran's most important non-oil resource in terms of international trade.

INDUSTRIES

Prerevolutionary industries ranged from food processing to iron and steel production and automobile assembly. During the shah's regime, joint ventures with foreign corporations resulted in the transfer of some Western technology and in training programs for Iranian laborers and managers. Following the 1979 revolution, industrial production suffered greatly. Among the disruptions were political conditions, a shortage of spare parts, an unreliable labor force, emigration of many capable industrial managers, and the war with Iraq. When the war with Iraq ended, industrial production gradually began to rebound.

Petroleum and refining remain the country's main industry. Iran is a key member of the Organization of Petroleum Exporting Countries (OPEC). It has nine oil refineries with a total capacity of 1.2 million barrels per day. The largest is in Abadan, near the border with Iraq. During the 1980 Iraqi invasion, this refinery was nearly destroyed, and its 400,000-barrel-per-day production ceased. By the late 1980s, however, the refinery resumed full production. Other major refineries are located in Esfahan, Bander-e Abbas, and Tehran.

Iran also has many important non-oil-related industries. They include the manufacture of textiles, food processing, sugar refining, iron and steel milling, and automobile assembly. Additionally, there is production of petrochemicals, fertilizer, cement, building materials, and machine tools. The country also produces a variety of household items and appliances, beverages, cigarettes, inlaid items, decorated ceramic tiles, and Persian rugs and carpets.

The Tehran metropolitan area, including Karaj, is the country's largest industrial core. It is home to most of the automobile assembly plants, household appliance factories, and clothing factories. Esfahan, in central Iran, is the second-largest industrial center, containing the country's major iron and steel plants. Esfahan is also particularly famous for its artisans, who create its hand-knotted carpets and artistically decorated metal household items, such as brass and copper trays. Tabriz is the industrial center of northwest Iran, producing tractors and other major machine tools. Iran's largest aluminum smelter is located in Arak. Many Iranian cities in addition to Esfahan are known for their carpet production; among the most important ones are Tabriz, Kerman, Nain, Qom, Kashan, Mashhad, and Hamadan.

NUCLEAR CRISIS

Perhaps the most controversial Iranian industry is its nuclear program. It is ironic that the United States, which is deeply concerned about Iran's nuclear program, was the main advocate of developing a nuclear program in Iran during the early 1970s when the shah, an American ally, was in power. Iran was supposed to build a nuclear plant to generate 23,000 megawatts of power. In 1974, the Atomic Energy Organization of Iran was established, and its aim was to construct about 40 reactors. The Iranian nuclear program, approved by the United States at the time, included technologies critical for construction of nuclear weapons. Knowing the shah's vast appetite for modern armaments, it was obvious that building weapons was part of the program.

When the 1979 revolution occurred, the country's attention was diverted from the nuclear program. Soon thereafter, however, Iran was invaded by Iraq in 1980. During the whole Iran-Iraq crisis, Iranians were astonished to see how the

Western world remained silent about this obvious aggression by Iraq. The West even remained silent when Iraqis used Western-made chemicals as weapons (of mass destruction) against Iranians. The silence of the world, especially the West, made some within the Iranian government think about returning to a nuclear program. Developing nuclear capability, they believed, would protect Iran against possible future aggression.

While Rafsanjani was a candid advocate of the nuclear program during his presidency, the program hardly made any progress. By 1996, Iran was able to make a deal with Russians to reconstruct the Bushehr plant. The Iranian nuclear program, however, became a global issue in 2002 when a political opposition group revealed the construction of an enrichment facility in Natanz, a city south of Tehran. The plant contained 160 centrifuges, with a project to increase it to 50,000 in the near future. Iran was also developing plutonium capabilities and building a heavy-water facility in Esfahan and some other plants in the nearby city of Arak. By the end of Khatami's presidency in 2005, the country was well on its way to becoming self-sufficient in nuclear technology.

Being a member of the Nuclear Non-Proliferation Treaty (NPT), Iran believes that it is entitled to nuclear technology. Many Iranian leaders like Ahmadinejad believe that the United States and the affluent Western countries are not really worried about Iran's nuclear weapons. They, after all, have the power to retaliate many times over. What the West is worried about, they believe, is the possible loss of the monopoly of technologies of the future that may replace fossil fuels. Further, Ahmadinejad believes that the United States and its Western allies want to preserve a divided world characterized by the rich industrial West and poor non-Western countries.

Most Iranians agree with Ahmadinejad in regard to the country's nuclear program. To them, Iran's accomplishments in the area of nuclear technology are a source of national pride.

Further, they believe that Iran is as much entitled to possessing nuclear technology (including nuclear weapons) as are the United States and its allies. What Iran may really be seeking is a freeze on and possible destruction of nuclear weapons worldwide. Iran feels threatened because Israel, Pakistan, and India, within the region, all have nuclear weapons.

The cat-and-mouse game over Iran's nuclear ambitions, however, continues between powerful Western nations and Iran. The new UN economic sanctions against Iran, which were approved in mid-2010, are the latest episode of this ongoing play. It is often argued that an energy-rich country like Iran does not need nuclear plants. What is obvious to Iranians, however, is the fact that fossil fuels are nonrenewable sources of energy. When they are gone, they are gone. So any country with a clear vision for the future would try to develop more durable and cleaner sources of energy to replace fossil fuels. And to Iranians, at least, nuclear energy seems to be a good choice for the future.

AGRICULTURE

Although only 10 percent of Iranian land is arable (suited to farming), agriculture still employs about a quarter of the labor force and accounts for one-fifth of the GDP. In a dry region such as the Middle East, Iran has managed to become a significant producer of crops and livestock. In fact, agriculture was the fastest-growing sector of the Iranian economy during much of 1990s. Crops are produced both through dry farming (rainfed) and irrigation schemes. Forms of irrigation include diverting river water through a network of canals, digging deep wells, and the qanat system. Qanats have been a significant source of water for crop production in the arid regions of Iran.

Today, Iran is the Middle East's leading producer of oranges, dates, melons, sheep, goats, and chickens. Wheat, barley, and rice are the major Iranian crops. While wheat and barley are produced almost all over the country in both rainfed and irrigated areas, rice production is limited to moist

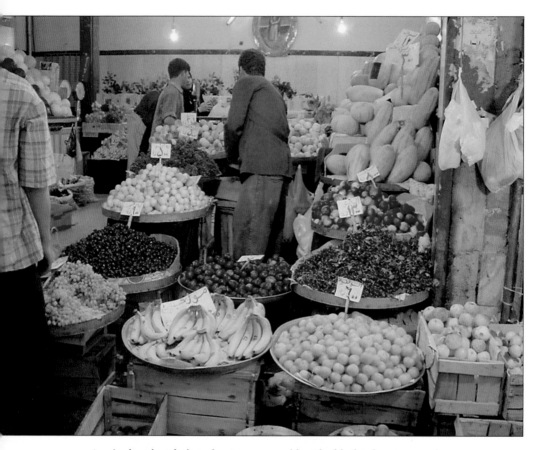

Iran's abundant fruit and nut crops provide valuable food sources and are exported throughout the world. Crops are among the most important Iranian exports. In an Iranian fruit market like this one, you can find grapes, peaches, plums, figs, melons, and a range of other delicious items.

areas bordering the Caspian Sea. Other crops include cotton, sugar beets, tea, cumin, hemp, tobacco, and saffron. Due to its large and growing population, Iran must import a significant amount of food, particularly wheat and rice.

Tree crops are also common in Iran. The country leads the world in production of pistachio nuts. Varieties of pistachios are

produced in different regions of Iran. Among other nuts produced are almonds, walnuts, and hazelnuts. Nuts and dried fruits
are among the most important Iranian export in terms of value.
Due to abundant sunshine, Iranian fruits are very tasty. Iranians
who live in other countries cannot wait to visit their homeland
in summertime to taste the variety of delicious grapes, peaches,
plums, oranges, figs, sweet and sour cherries, mulberries, and
several varieties of sweet melons.

LIVESTOCK, FISHING, AND FORESTRY

Pastures adequate to support livestock herds cover 27 percent
of Iran's total land area. Sheep, goats, and cattle grazing in
green pastures are a common sight that a traveler through Iran
is sure to notice. Besides meat, animals are used for their milk,
wool, and hides. Manure is used as fertilizer and dried for use
as fuel in rural villages.

Fishing is mainly done in the Caspian Sea, along the Persian
Gulf coast, and in the Gulf of Oman. Fish caught in the Persian
Gulf and the Gulf of Oman includes sardines, sole, tuna, snap-
per, and swordfish. Shrimp also are taken from these waters. The
Caspian Sea is known for its supply of whitefish, white salmon,
carp, bream, pike, catfish, and sturgeon. Sturgeon is a valuable
fish, since it is the source of the roe that is processed into caviar.
Iran is one of the world's largest suppliers of caviar, and Iranian
caviar is recognized as being the finest in the world. Caviar, along
with the spice saffron, are luxury items that visitors to Iran often
take back with them to their families and friends.

Forestry has been an important land use, particularly along
the northern slopes of the Elburz Mountains. Due to abundant
rainfall and mild climate there, dense forests cover these slopes.
Caspian forests include hardwoods such as oak, beech, maple,
elm, ash, walnut, fig, and alder. There are also forests covering
the western slopes of the Zagros Mountains and the slopes of
Khorasan Province. With the exception of Turkey, Iran has the
only commercially productive forests in the Middle East.

TRANSPORTATION

Iran serves as a bridge connecting Europe, Central Asia, and the Caucasus with the Persian Gulf and Indian Ocean to the south. Although Iran's mountainous nature makes construction of national roads and railroads difficult and costly, the country does have a relatively well-established transportation network. A systematic highway network connects most major cities. It also connects to the roads in neighboring countries to the north, east, and west. There are about 110,000 miles (177,000 kilometers) of roads, of which 1,360 miles (2,189 kilometers) are highways with at least four lanes.

With its long coastlines along the Persian Gulf, Gulf of Oman, and Caspian Sea, Iran contains many ports. The major southern ports include Shaheed Rajayee, with an annual capacity of 13 million tons (11.7 million metric tons), and Shaheed Beheshti and Bushehr, each with a capacity of 2 million tons (1.8 million metric tons). Among major ports along the Caspian Sea are Anzali and Nowshahr, both with a capacity of 1.0 to 1.5 million tons (0.9 to 1.4 million metric tons). According to Iranian government figures, the country's annual port capacity is about 42 million tons (38.1 million metric tons). More than 4,300 miles (6,920 kilometers) of railroad track connect these ports to other Iranian cities. Iran's shipping lines and the National Oil Tanker Company are among the world's leading marine carriers.

Iran is also well connected to the rest of the world through airways. There are more than 300 airports, about 130 of which have paved runways. Mehrabad Airport near Tehran is the nation's largest in terms of carriers, flights, and passengers.

TRADE AND TRADE PARTNERS

As has been mentioned before, petroleum is Iran's major export. It accounted for some 80 percent of the country's $70 billion export trade during 2009. Customers vary from year to year, although the most reliable are Japan, China, India, Italy,

South Korea, Turkey, and the United Arab Emirates. Other significant exports include carpets, fruits and nuts (pistachio, raisins, and dates), chemical and petrochemical products, animal hides, caviar, textiles, garments, and other food products.

Major imports include industrial machinery, iron and steel products, transport equipment, foodstuffs (mainly grains), textiles, pharmaceuticals, chemical products, and technical services. The total value of imports for the year 2009 was around $57 billion. Major import partners are the United Arab Emirates, China, India, South Korea, Russia, France, and Italy. Due to U.S. economic sanctions against Iranian goods, there is no major trade between the two nations.

ENVIRONMENTAL PROBLEMS

Iranian cities, particularly large metropolitan areas such as Tehran, Esfahan, and Tabriz, suffer from a variety of environmental problems caused by transportation and industrial pollution. Air pollution, especially in Tehran, is the most serious human-made environmental problem. Primary sources include vehicle emissions, refinery operations, and industrial plants. The level of lead concentration in Tehran's air is so high that occasionally the government asks citizens to stay inside or wear masks for safety. Pollution related to oil production in the Persian Gulf areas also is a significant problem. Soil erosion and depletion are widespread, due to overgrazing and inefficient agricultural practices. Deforestation also has become a problem, due to illegal cutting and inadequate forest management. Other problems relating to the natural environment include earthquakes, droughts, floods, sandstorms and dust storms, and water shortages.

Family is the foundation of the Iranian lifestyle. Marriage is considered a contract between two families. The actions of one member can impact the reputation of an entire family.

9

Living in Iran Today

Iranian society is becoming more and more divided in several ways. It is a society characterized by religious groups versus secular factions; urban dwellers versus rural population; traditional beliefs versus a Westernized outlook; and finally, rich versus poor. All of these groups, however, do have one thing in common: the importance of family. In the West, the individual tends to be the focus of society. In Iran, as elsewhere in the Middle East, society and societal laws focus much more on the family.

THE FAMILY

Family forms the basic unit of Iranian society. The unit is defined by a series of principles that are recognized by most Iranians even when they live abroad. The father is usually the head of the household. He is responsible for the family's well-being. This goes beyond merely financial support; he is responsible for family members' social and spiritual needs as well. He is the authority and disciplinarian of the house, so he demands obedience. Since other family members look up to him, the father must be a good role model. If he goes "astray" in some way, the entire family will suffer the consequences.

Of course, this latter tradition is also true for the mother. The mother is especially considered a role model for daughters. She is very much the moral gauge of the family. She is supposed to raise good children and instill good values in them. The Prophet Muhammad said, "Heaven is at the feet of mothers." This saying and many similar proverbs and comments found in Iranian secular and religious literature have greatly elevated the status of mothers in Iranian society. Usually when a woman reaches the status of a mother, she is much more respected by others. The great importance placed on motherhood has put a lot of pressure on childless women.

Officially, Islam allows men to marry up to four wives, and the new Islamic government has made it easier for Iranian men to do so. This has created hot debates among Iranian intellectuals. The Qu'ran emphasizes that a man who decides to marry more than one wife should be able to treat them equally. But it also notes that this is often impossible. Some critics of the practice believe that a systematic interpretation of Islamic verses discourages polygamy. Although allowed, however, polygamy is rarely practiced today in Iran. Traditionally there has been a stigma attached to the practice, and educated men rarely choose multiple wives. Today, some women even put a clause relating to polygamy in their marriage agreement, indicating that the husband cannot have another wife.

MARRIAGE

How do Iranian youth find their mates? It really depends on the social, economic, and religious status of their families. Among traditional families, especially in smaller towns and rural areas, it is customary that the family of the groom finds a prospective bride for him. Of course, there are various criteria for selecting a suitable mate. Usually the mate is chosen from a similar socioeconomic class and religious background. The family's reputation in the neighborhood is the most important factor in bride selection and, for that matter, in the groom's desirability as well. Chances of finding a husband from a decent family are significantly reduced, for example, if the proposed bride's mother does not have a good reputation.

If the reputation of the bride's family somehow matches that of the groom's family, then the parents of the groom (mainly the female members such as mother, sister, and aunts) visit the bride's house. Here the family of the bride has to be on its best behavior so that the groom's family will leave their house with a good impression. Among the things that the groom's family are concerned with are the cleanliness of the house, good taste in decoration, the quality of service given to guests, and, of greatest importance, the family's mannerisms and level of politeness.

Of course, during this meeting the family of the bride also scrutinizes the family of their potential son-in-law. Toward the end of the meeting, through their conversation and mannerisms, the parties indicate whether they are willing to hold a future meeting. If there is a mutual liking between the two families, the groom's family requests another meeting. The next meeting could be outside the house with chaperones or another visit to the bride's house. The couple is given an opportunity to converse and find out about each other. If things go well, the next step is the engagement, usually a small ceremony held in the presence of the couple's close family and friends. If things still progress positively, marriage usually takes place a year or two later. The size of the wedding celebration depends on the socioeconomic status of the families involved.

Arranged marriages occur less frequently among middle- and upper-class educated families. As is the case in the West, couples often meet at parties or at public places such as colleges, parks, or movie theaters. When there is a clear mutual attraction and interest, then the parents become involved in conducting formalities.

Marriages are conducted by the Shiite clerics or by licensed individuals. Unlike Christian marriage ceremonies, which usually are conducted in a church, Iranian Muslim marriages are not done in mosques (Muslim churches). Muslims are encouraged to marry Muslims. They cannot marry people who practice polytheistic religions. A Muslim woman can only marry a Muslim man (although he may be a convert to the faith). Muslim men, however, can marry women of other monotheistic religions such as Christianity, Judaism, or Zoroastrianism. In multireligious marriages, the marriage has to be conducted in Islamic fashion and the non-Muslim spouse takes a Muslim name.

Marriage is a contract between the two families. There is always *mahreyyeh* (money or property deed), which can be loosely translated as the bride's price. After some preliminary negotiations, elders of the two families agree on the amount of mahreyyeh. It can be in cash, gold coins, or a deed to certain properties. The size of mahreyyeh again depends on the socio-economic status of the families involved. The rationale behind mahreyyeh is to secure the bride's status in the groom's house. In the case of divorce initiated by a husband, he must transfer mahreyyeh to the wife.

Mahreyyeh legally belongs to the wife, and she can cash it anytime during the marriage at her request. Traditionally, however, it is transferred to the wife only in cases of divorce or the husband's death or disappearance. Some women choose to use it for the education of their children. In the Iranian legal system, women and men can both initiate divorce, but usually this step is much easier for the husband to initiate than the wife.

STATUS OF WOMEN

Compared with their counterparts in Arab countries, Iranian women have achieved significant rights. They are generally well-educated and have occupied many professional positions traditionally filled by men. Many government clerics do not believe in the equality of men and women, but the assertiveness of Iranian women, supported by some enlightened clerics like President Khatami, has paved the way for women's further professional achievement. In a speech, Khatami indicated that according to Islam there is no difference between men and women. To prove his statement he selected Masoumeh Ebtekar, an Iranian woman educated in the United States, as one of his vice presidents.

Women were very influential in the election of Khatami, both in 1997 and 2001. They campaigned and voted for Khatami and other reformist parliamentary candidates. Recently, another popular ayatollah also publicly declared that there should be nothing to stop women from becoming president or even the supreme religious leader. This statement was very significant, because the position of Supreme Leader is believed to be ordained by God. There are many prominent female professionals in Iran who have significantly contributed to advance the process of development forward, and some have served in very important governmental positions like ministers and parliament members. Many serve as educators in Iranian universities, filmmakers, artists, and human-rights activists. A good example of an active human-rights activist is Shirin Ebadi, the former judge and current attorney who in 2003 also was the first Muslim woman to win the Noble Peace Prize.

Despite all the progress, under Iranian law women still are not exactly equal to men. There are a number of discriminatory laws that female activists and their supporters would like to change. For example, a woman's testimony in court is worth

Activist Shirin Ebadi (*pictured here in 2005*) was awarded the Nobel Peace Prize in 2003 for her efforts to promote democracy and human rights—particularly for women and children—in the Middle East.

only half that of a man's, and in terms of blood money (paid when a person is murdered or killed by accident), the value of a woman's life is half of a man's. Women also are no longer allowed to be judges, but they can be attorneys at the court. But the most discriminatory law relates to child custody and distribution of wealth in cases of divorce or death of a husband. Often, men get custody unless children are very young. And in the case of a husband's death, the husband's father, rather than his wife, can get the custody of children and authority over his son's assets.

Many Iranian women also complain about the strict dress codes that have been imposed on them by the government since the 1979 revolution. Before the revolution, women could appear in public in Western dress. Whether or not to wear the traditional Islamic head veil was a personal choice. Under the new government, women are only allowed to display their face, hands, and toes in public. In larger cities, most women wear scarves and loose garments to cover their body. The preference of the government's moral police, however, is the chador, a tentlike veil covering the body from head to toe. Women, however, do not always observe dress rules, and they are frequently stopped and warned by the cruising moral police in public places.

ART AND LITERATURE

Although in the West, Iran is known for its political upheavals and revolutionary fervor, most Iranians see politics as an ever-changing wave. They simply try to adjust as well as they can. Meanwhile, like everybody else, they live their daily lives and try to fulfill their spiritual needs as well as their material necessities. Perhaps the most obvious aesthetic face of Iranian culture is its art and poetry. Iranians have a deep appreciation of art. Seeing a beautiful Persian carpet with delicate coloring and design, a ceramic bowl with exquisite patterns, a charming miniature painting decorated by delightful calligraphy, or an attractive garden will stimulate their artistic senses and add to the quality of their lives.

The American scholar Arthur Pope, in his six-volume classic, *A Survey of Persian Art*, eloquently explains Persian art and architecture. Pope spent a good portion of his life in Iran and was taken by the architectural beauty of the numerous mosques and palaces that he visited. A beautiful blue dome against a brownish mountain in the background is an image that an artistic mind will not easily forget. Many Iranians who live abroad crave returning home to see once again the beautiful places of their past memories. They long to see the majestic Persepolis in the sunset, the mosques and palaces of Esfahan, and the shrine of Imam Reza in Mashhad. They dream of cruising on the mysterious and puzzling waters of the Alisadr caverns around Hamadan, spending a summer evening on the slopes of Darband in northern Tehran, and contemplating the tombs of Hafez and Sadi, their favorite Iranian poets, while quietly whispering their poems.

Iranian works of art are not always kept in museums. They are also displayed in public for the enjoyment of passersby. City squares may have posters that include poems written in exquisite Persian calligraphy and accompanied by beautiful paintings or drawings. The content of most of the displayed poetry is about love and spiritual maturity. Far from being political, these posters display the poetic heart of the nation.

POETRY

To those who are familiar with the world's poetic and romantic literature, Iran is known as the "land of flowers and nightingales." Numerous Iranian poets have written sizzling tales of love affairs between legendary lovers. This love is often compared symbolically to the unconditional love of the nightingale for the flower, or the sacrificial passion of the moth for the flame. Long before Shakespeare wrote his masterpiece *Romeo and Juliet*, the famous Iranian poet Nezami (died A.D. 1202) wrote his sensational tale of Leili and Majnon, the two lovers from conflicting social, economic, and political backgrounds who struggled to save their love against all odds. It is possible that the romantic tale of Leili and Majnon was Shakespeare's inspiration for writing his celebrated *Romeo and Juliet*.

There are many other romantic tales from various periods of Iranian literary history that are among the most commonly read literature by the Iranian population. Today, many Iranians seek refuge in the warmth of the uplifting and mediating poetry of Hafez (died A.D. 1389), the legendary Iranian poet whose work is used in the art of fortune-telling.

The Iranian poets most widely read in the United States are Rumi (died A.D. 1273), known for his insightful Sufi poetry, and Omar Khayyam (died A.D. 1131) for his enriching philosophical poetry. In reality, Rumi has remained the most read foreign poet in the United States for more than a decade. His work can be found in the form of books and audiotapes in any major bookstore. The impact of poetry on Iranian culture is so staggering that one can listen to an everyday conversation among Iranians and hear lines of poetry used in their expressions and arguments.

Iran is also a land of great scientists and philosophers. Among them were Khwarazmi, Razi, and Avicenna. Khwarazmi, a ninth-century mathematician and astronomer, wrote the first work of algebra. The word *algebra* is derived from his books; the word *algorithm* comes from a distortion of his name. Zakareyya Razi, a great scientist and physician living between the ninth and tenth centuries, is known for his discovery of alcohol and his books on curing smallpox and measles. Ibn Sina (Avicenna) lived between the tenth and eleventh centuries and wrote more than 200 books, including *The Canon of Medicine*, an encyclopedia summarizing all the known medical knowledge at the time from across the world. This work, through its translated versions, remained the most influential book of medicine in the world until the seventeenth century.

The Iranian cultural landscape today is dotted with the tombs and shrines of famous poets, writers, scientists, and philosophers. They far outnumber the shrines of politicians and military figures.

CINEMA

Iranian artists and intellectuals have also shown their creativity in areas of the modern arts. Iranian cinema is considered to be among the world's most progressive. Prerevolutionary cinema was very popular in Iran, and some Iranian movies managed to win international awards, even though Iranian cinema was not yet globally known. The postrevolutionary Iranian cinema, however, has captured the world's attention. Every year, several Iranian movies win awards from the most respectable film festivals, and they are played in theaters around the world. In major American cities, Iranian films are shown frequently, and in some cases there are film festivals focusing on the work of successful Iranian directors.

Cinema has become a medium in which Iranian intellectuals can express their fears and aspirations and share their stories with their countrymen and the rest of the world. It has become a way of diffusing Iranian culture to other parts of the world. Many Americans who saw Majid Majidi's tender movie *Children of Heaven* talked for weeks about the impoverished little Ali and Zahra, the brother and sister who had to share the same pair of sneakers. This cinematic tale was one of the five candidates for the 1999 Academy Award for Best Foreign Film. In 1997, Kiarostami's *Taste of Cherry*, the story of despair over Iran's social structure, won the first-place Palm d'Or award at the international Cannes Film Festival. In 2000, three Iranian movies won prizes at Cannes; one of them was *Apple*, a movie by Samira Makhmalbaf, a 20-year-old Iranian woman. She was the youngest award winner in the festival's history. Some of the most recent successful Iranian movies are *The Song of Sparrows, Santouri (The Music Man), Ceasefire, Lizard, In the Name of Father, Offside, Crimson Gold, Transit Cafe, Weeping Willow,* and *Women Prison.*

Today there are more than 20 directors whose movies have captured the attention of their colleagues throughout the world. Among them are Tahmine Milani and Rakhshan Banni-Etemad, both of whom have been particularly successful in demonstrating the problems of Iranian women and society at large under the Islamic Republic's government. Milani has been imprisoned by the regime for her aggressive criticism of government policies. Her movies, especially *Two Women* and *The Hidden Half*, have been praised by many throughout the world. It is interesting that the Islamic government at first promoted the motion picture industry for propaganda purposes. Today, however, the industry has become one of the most outspoken critics of government policies. Although intellectual movies are not always successful at the local box office, young people from high schools, colleges, and universities are among the regular viewers.

SPORTS

Sports have always been popular in Iran. There are tales of Iranian youth competing with Greeks during ancient Olympics. Among traditional sports practiced in Iran are horseback riding, wrestling, fencing, archery, and polo. Today, the most popular sports are soccer (called football in Iran), weight lifting, and different styles of wrestling. Iranian wrestlers are among the best in the world, and they have won many medals in international competitions. The Iranian national soccer team is one of the best in Asia, and many Iranian athletes play for European professional teams.

EDUCATION

Another success story of postrevolutionary Iran has been its educational system. Educating the public has been a government priority. Today, an estimated 70 to 80 percent of Iranians can read, and almost all children go to school. Public schools are free. In Iran, however, private schools often provide students with a better-quality education. There are national standard tests that primary, middle, and high school students must pass in order to move to the next level.

Admission to college or university can be difficult. Although the number of institutions of higher education has increased since the revolution, so has the college-age population. There simply is not enough space for all young people seeking to further their education. Applicants must take a difficult entrance exam, called "the conquer." High school students devote much of their last two years preparing for this exam. Newspapers publish the test results in midsummer. Those long, hot days before the announcement of results are known as "days of destiny" for many Iranian youth. Those who fail the test usually

Iran's postrevolutionary educational system has achieved great successes. Iran's public schools have boosted the country's literacy rate to about 80 percent. Students must successfully pass nationally standardized tests in the primary, middle, and high schools in order to move ahead to the next step in their education.

try the next calendar year. If they fail again, they must do their two-year compulsory military service, which is required for Iranian males when they reach 21 years of age.

IRANIAN CALENDAR

The Iranian calendar is based on solar activity. The year begins at the spring equinox, when the length of day and night are equal throughout the world. Since it takes the Earth 365 days,

5 hours, 49 minutes, and 4 seconds to complete one revolution around the sun, the Iranian New Year does not fall on the same day every year; it moves between March 19 and March 22.

The Iranian calendar also displays the Islamic nature of Iran. It is called Hejri-e Shamsi, meaning the solar calendar based on migration. Year one of this calendar is A.D. 622, the year that the Prophet Muhammad migrated from Mecca to Medina in the Arabian Peninsula, where he established the first Islamic community. The official Iranian week starts on Saturday and ends on Friday. According to Muslims, God created Earth in six days and rested on Friday, so Friday became the Muslim holiday. Iranians usually take Thursday afternoon off, to make a longer weekend. On Thursday evening, many Iranian Muslims visit cemeteries and pray for their deceased relatives and friends.

NO-ROOZ

No-Rooz is the greatest Persian festival for Iranians throughout the world. The name comes from *no*, meaning "new," and *rooz*, meaning "day," or New Day. It is a joyous celebration of nature's rejuvenation. The long, cold winter has passed and spring, the season of rebirth, has arrived. Iranians have celebrated this 13-day festival for some 3,000 years. On the thirteenth day, families go picnicking in open fields. Young men and women tie the grass, hoping that by the time the knot is open they will meet their future mates. Although Persian in origin, No-Rooz is celebrated by nearly all Iranian cultures.

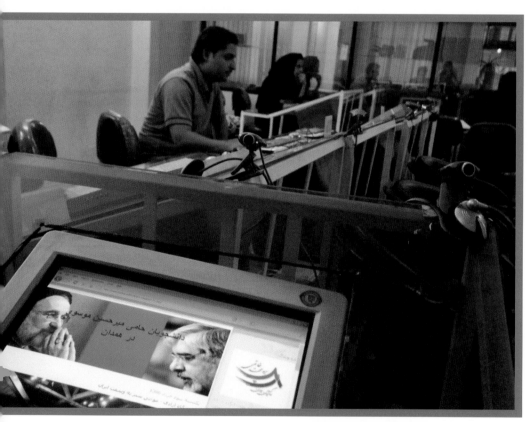

A computer in an Internet café in Tehran displays a Web site for reformist candidate Mir Hussein Mousavi *(right)*. The reformists used the Internet to mobilize their supporters, taking advantage of media not controlled by the government.

CHAPTER

10

Iran Looks Ahead

uzzing Tehran, Iran's populous capital with its 8.5 million
people, is one of the busiest cities of the world. It is a city of
contrasts. Wide boulevards, highways, and metros in the newly
expanded city stand in sharp contrast to the narrow winding streets
of the old quarters. The city leaves a variety of visual impressions in
the minds of visitors. New skyscrapers imitating the architectural
designs of the West stand in marked contrast to old courtyard houses
characterizing traditional folk architecture of the Middle East. Snow-
capped peaks limit the northern expansion of the city but provide
Tehran with a splendid year-round view. In winter, ski resorts along
the hillsides are popular attractions for skiers and people who simply
want to get out of the crowded city and breathe fresh mountain air.

Billboards and pictures posted on walls facing streets and highways tell of the country's recent turbulent history. Revolutionary

propaganda, sponsored mainly by the government, still can be seen all over the city. There are pictures of revolutionary clerics who have held political positions at various times during the postrevolutionary period. There are photos of many martyrs of the bloody Iran-Iraq War, which took the lives of several hundred thousand young Iranian and Iraqi men. And, of course, there are anti-American slogans and propaganda that attest to the Islamic Republic's defiance of perceived American imperialistic intentions. All of these are visual reminders of the political changes that have occurred in Iran since the 1979 revolution.

The famous slogan of the revolution, "Neither East, nor West," is still seen on the walls. The East, meaning today's Russia, has been neutralized over time. The giant country no longer seems intent on spreading Communism and conquering neighboring lands. The Iranian government, however, is still suspicious of the United States—the West. With American military operations in Afghanistan and Iraq, Iranian officials are nervous. They see Iran as the next possible American target since the country was included as one of George W. Bush's "Axis of Evil" nations.

Although many Iranians dislike the current regime in Iran, they despise the idea of another foreign intervention. They have not forgotten that their dreams of freedom and democratic government were crushed by the American CIA-supported coup of 1953. As a result, Iranians realized that foreign countries look out for their own national interests. Thus, if political change is needed, they believe, it should come from within the country itself, and within the guidelines of its ruling system. America's unconditional support of the shah at the expense of Iranian people's freedom created a negative image of the U.S. government in the minds of Iranian intellectuals. Dissatisfaction with the shah's government inevitably led to a nationwide uprising that eventually forced the shah out of Iran and paved the way for the current Islamic Republic.

Today, about three decades after the revolution, the country faces a variety of social, political, and economic problems. Though there have been improvements in the lives of rural people and public education and health, the government's overwhelming corruption and disrespect for democracy have disappointed countless Iranian citizens, many of whom were once revolutionary sympathizers. Many people do not like the government's strict implementation of Islamic dress codes for women and sexual segregation of youth in public. There is also widespread concern about the increasing political oppression of intellectuals. The shortage of job opportunities has created an atmosphere of uncertainty and mistrust that far overshadows lingering anti-American feelings. Widespread dissatisfactions with the status quo resulted in mass demonstrations throughout the country during the summer of 2009. They followed a controversial presidential election victory for incumbent president Ahmadinejad.

The crisis took the world by surprise. It projected a flashback to three decades earlier, when another generation of young Iranians brought down the pro-American regime of Mohammad Reza Pahlavi, which was replaced by the Islamic Republic. The revolutionary government promised among many other things an egalitarian society, freedom of expression, and a government dedicated to democracy and transparency. Today, an examination of the 30-year legacy of the Islamic Republic does not indicate that any of those major promises have been fulfilled. In some areas, such as gender equality and narrowing the gap between rich and poor, not only has there not been significant progress, but the country has actually regressed. This growing gap between the promises and the dim realities has gradually created an atmosphere of hopelessness and depression. Frustrations finally erupted in mass demonstrations following a controversial election.

Today, there are almost twice as many Iranians as there were at the time of the 1979 revolution. More than half of the population has been born since the revolution. They have no memory of sacrifices that their parents made to supposedly improve the Iranian political system and Iranian life. Many of these young people today are facing a range of problems, including high unemployment, high inflation, nonaffordable housing, and above all a police state that is intervening in their private affairs by telling them what to wear, what to say, what to believe, whom to be with, what music to listen to—in short, how to live. Thanks to significant advances in the areas of health, education, and technology, these young people are well educated about the world. When they compare their lives with young people elsewhere, they feel left out. They crave their basic human rights such as freedom, democracy, and social justice. Some tend to overcome their frustrations by finding refuge in narcotics, which are readily and cheaply available in streets of major cities. Others are indifferent, and still others voice their opinions when circumstances such as the June 2009 election events called for it.

During the election campaigns, many young and educated Iranians felt their fears and aspirations were understood by their favorite presidential candidate, Mir Hussein Mousavi. The candidate broke a taboo by campaigning hand-in-hand with his well-educated and highly respected wife. For many liberal-minded Iranians, especially women, it was truly refreshing to see Mousavi appearing with his wife and campaigning about improving the status of women in a country that has treated women as second-class citizens. Women have been held back by discriminatory laws in areas such as criminal law, family inheritance, court witnessing, divorce, and child custody. One of his campaign promises, which was popular with the youth, was to call for removal of the "moral police" from the streets. The harassment by the moral police has significantly increased since Ahmadinejad became president in 2005. Mousavi's candidacy somehow managed to bring a sense of hope for a better future for women, the young, and the middle class.

The author sensed an unusual optimism and a fervent hope for changes when visiting with relatives, friends, and colleagues during a visit to Iran a few weeks before the 2009 election. The feeling of anger, frustration, apathy, and disillusionment seemed to have been replaced by an optimistic sense of hope mainly inspired by the candidacy of Mousavi. Most individuals with whom the author interacted in Tehran and elsewhere indicated a preference for Mousavi. Also, a scientific poll taken a week or so before the actual election showed Mousavi to be the clear front-runner with 54 percent of the votes (compared with 24 percent for Ahmadinejad.) So, the election result, as announced by the Interior Ministry, came as a shock to millions of Iranians, who poured onto the streets in protest of the results.

Iranians face an uncertain future. The problems enumerated above are causing many Iranian youth to consider leaving the country—particularly for the United States. It is evident that the political billboards do not necessarily exemplify the fears and aspirations of all Tehran residents.

Some recent Iranian motion picture themes express the frustration of Iranian youth in the face of unnecessary harassment by the government's moral police. A 2007-released Iranian movie, *Santouri (The Music Man)* presents a tragic tale of a young Iranian couple crushed by unjust social laws. A young, talented songwriter and singer is not allowed to publish his CDs or perform publicly due to unfair government laws. His dreams shattered, he ends up unemployed and depressed. His deep depression leads him to narcotics, which ruins his self-esteem and destroys his once loving relations with his wife. His frustrated wife, not finding any reason to stay in Iran, leaves her home and family, and like many other young Iranians, chooses to live in a foreign land.

Many thoughtful Iranians are puzzled about the government's unnecessary preoccupation with the behavior of youth while the country is suffering from serious economic and social problems. The Iranian currency has depreciated more than 100 times since prerevolutionary times. A U.S. dollar was worth 7 Iranian tomans in 1979; now, the dollar is worth about 1,000 tomans.

Currently, more than 50 percent of the country's population is under 27 years of age. This population "bomb" is more threatening to hard-liners in power than is any foreign threat. These youths, along with Iranian women, want an aggressive president and parliament that stand for the rule of law. They want to see the government become more democratic and less theocratic. A country with such vast natural and human resources, if managed well, can become one of the world's most prosperous nations.

In the age of globalization, Iranians do not feel as isolated as they once did. Now satellites and the Internet have reached even remote areas of the country. Thanks to the industriousness of young Iranians, Internet cafés are all over larger cities. During the June 2009 crisis, when the government prevented journalists from covering the news, demonstrators and their sympathizers managed to report the news to the rest of the world via their cell phones and computers. Due to improved communications, Iranians can easily contact their 3 million relatives who live abroad. Many of the 1 million Iranians who live in the United States regularly visit Iran or are in touch via telephone, computer, or satellite TV. In fact, many Iranian TV and radio stations broadcast from the United States and are viewed or heard by Iranians inside Iran. Similarly, Iranians in the United States are able to watch Iranian TV broadcasts. Many Iranian children living in American cities are learning to speak Farsi by watching children's programs televised from Tehran through state-run Iranian television.

In this age of information and connectivity, Iranians feel their concerns are being heard and seen by the rest of the world. They desperately want to prove that they belong to the global community of nations and do not stand for terrorism and lawlessness. Many young Iranians, for example, held a candlelight vigil in the streets of Tehran for the victims of the September 11, 2001, terrorist attacks in the United States. These young Iranians identify with a compassionate and caring Iran—a country that produced great scientists, philosophers, and poets like Sadi, whose words decorate the entrance to the UN building in New York City. His wisdom still resonates with people wherever one speaks of a united humanity. In the thirteenth century, Sadi wrote:

> The children of Adam are limbs of each other
> Having been created of one essence.
> When the calamity of time afflicts one limb
> The other limbs cannot remain at rest.
> If thou hast no sympathy for the troubles of others
> Thou art unworthy to be called by the name of a man.

Facts at a Glance

Official Name	Islamic Republic of Iran
Location	Middle East; southwest Asia; shares borders with Pakistan, Afghanistan, Turkmenistan, Azerbaijan, Armenia, Turkey, and Iraq
Area	636,296 square miles (1,648,000 square kilometers), three times the size of France
Climate	Diverse; mostly arid or semiarid, subtropical along Caspian Sea coast
Major Rivers	Karun, Dez, Karkheh, Sefidrud, Haraz
Major Mountains	Elburz Mountains, Damavand Summit: 18,605 feet (5,671 meters), Zagros Mountains
Natural Hazards	Periodic droughts, floods; dust storms, sandstorms; earthquakes
Environmental Problems	Air pollution from vehicle emissions, refinery operations, and industrial effluents; deforestation; overgrazing; desertification
Population	76,923,300 (2010 estimate); 68 percent living in cities (2008 estimate)
Natural Increase	1.25 percent (births: 18.5 per 1,000; deaths: 5.9 per 1,000, both for 2010)
Capital	Tehran (8.5 million population)
Cities (1,000,000+)	Mashhad, Esfahan, Tabriz, Shiraz
Ethnic Groups	Persian (51 percent), Azerbaijani (24 percent), Gilaki and Mazandarani (8 percent), Kurd (7 percent), Arab (3 percent), Lur (2 percent), Baloch (2 percent), Turkoman (2 percent), others (1 percent)
Religions	Shiite Muslim, 89 percent; Sunni Muslim, 10 percent; Zoroastrians, Jews, Christians, Bahais, 1 percent
Languages	Official language: Farsi (Persian); other languages: Kurdish, Turkish, Arabic, Lori, Gilaki, Mazandarani, Balochi
Literacy Rate	80 percent
Average Life Expectancy	69.8 years (male 68.3, female 71.3)
National Holiday	Islamic Republic Day, April 1 (1979)

Government

Form of Government	Theocratic Islamic Republic
Government Branches	Executive, Judicial, Legislative

Head of State	Ayatollah Seyyed Ali Khamenei, the Supreme Religious Leader
President	Mahmoud Ahmadinejad (second term in office)
Constitution	December 3, 1979 (major revisions, 1989)
Suffrage	At age 15; Iranian citizenship required

Economy

Natural Resources	Petroleum, natural gas, copper, coal, chromium, iron, zinc, lead, sulfur, manganese
Land Use	Arable land: 10 percent; permanent crops: 1 percent; permanent pastures: 27 percent; forests and woodland: 10 percent; other: 52 percent
Gross National Product	$827 billion U.S. based on PPP (2009 estimate)
Per Capita GDP	$12,500 U.S. based on PPP (2009 estimate)
Share of Sectors for GDP	11 percent agriculture, 45 percent industry, 44 percent services (2009 estimate)
Agricultural Products	Wheat, rice, other grains, sugar, beets, fruits, nuts, cotton, dairy products, wool, caviar
Industries	Petroleum, petrochemicals, textiles, cement and other building materials, food processing (particularly sugar refining and vegetable oil production), metal fabricating
Major Imports	Total $57 billion (2009): machinery, metalworks, foodstuffs, pharmaceuticals, technical services, chemical products, military supplies
Major Exports	Total $70 billion (year 2009): petroleum, carpets, fruits, dried fruits (pistachio, raisin, date), caviar, petrochemicals, textiles, garments, agricultural products, iron, and steel
Major Trading Partners	Japan, China, India, South Korea, Italy, France, United Arab Emirates (UAE), Turkey, Russia
Currency	Rial; Toman (10 Iranian Rials=1 Toman); $1=1,000 Tomans (2010)

3900 B.C.	Sialk (near Kashan), the first city on the Iranian Plateau, is built.
1500–800 B.C.	Persians and the Medes, two Aryan groups, enter Iranian Plateau.
1000 B.C.	Prophet Zoroaster introduces concepts of monotheism, duality of good and evil, angels, and heaven and hell.
550–330 B.C.	Achaemenid Empire: Cyrus the Great establishes the Persian Empire in 550 B.C.
334 B.C.	Alexander the Great invades Iran and burns the city of Persepolis.
323–141 B.C.	Seleucid dynasty is established by one of Alexander's generals.
247 B.C.–A.D. 224	Parthians defeat Greek Seleucids and rule over all of Persia.
A.D. 224–642	Sassanid Empire: Ardeshir I begins the dynasty.
642	Iran falls to Arab Islamic army.
661–750	Umayyad Caliphate rule; Iran is ruled by Arabs.
750–1258	Abbasid Caliphate; adopts Sassanid administration systems, establishes extensive bureaucracy, hires Persian viziers.
820–1220	The Golden Age of Iranian and Islamic scientists and philosophers.
1220	Genghis Khan and his Mongol hordes attack Iran.
1405	Timur (Tamerlane), a Turco-Mongol leader, conquers Iran.
1501–1524	Safavid dynasty: Shah Ismail I unites all of Persia under Iranian leadership.
1587–1629	Reign of Shah Abbas the Great marks the pinnacle of the Safavid dynasty.
1722	Mahmoud Afghan attacks Iran and captures Esfahan, ending the Safavids' rule.
1729–1747	Nader Shah expels the Afghans and reunites the country.
1750–1779	Karim Khan Zand gains control of Iran; he rejects being called shah or king.
1795–1925	Qajar dynasty: Qajars succeed in reuniting the country.
1813; 1828	Qajars lose the Caucasus (present-day Georgia, Armenia, and Azerbaijan) to the Russians in two separate treaties: the Gulistan in 1813 and the Turkmanchay in 1828.

1851–1906	Qajars lose central Asian provinces to the Russians and are forced to give up all claims on Afghanistan to the British.
1906	Constitutional Movement and establishment of Iran's first parliament, or Majles; the beginning of modern Iranian history.
1921	Reza Khan, an officer in the army, stages a coup against the last king of Qajar.
1925–1979	Pahlavi dynasty: Reza Shah strengthens the authority of the central government.
1941	Reza Shah abdicates in favor of his son and is deported to Johannesburg; Mohammad Reza Shah becomes the new king.
1951–1953	Mosaddeq era: nationalization of Iranian oil; shah leaves; CIA-supported coup brings shah back to power.
1962–1963	Shah introduces his White Revolution (land reform, workers' rights, and women's suffrage, among other initiatives).
1963–1973	Iran enjoys economic growth, prosperity, and political stability. Arab oil embargo quadruples Iran's oil revenues to $20 billion a year; more money brings more corruption and inequality, which leads to shah's fall.
1979	Ayatollah Khomeini returns to Iran after 14 years of exile.
	The Islamic Republic of Iran is proclaimed following a national referendum.
	Student militants attack American Embassy, taking Americans hostage.
1980	Banisadr is elected as the first president of the Islamic Republic.
	Iraqi army invades Iran to annex Shatt al-Arab.
1981	American hostages in Iran are released after 444 days of captivity.
1988	The 290 passengers of an Iran Airbus airliner are shot down by the USS *Vincennes*.
	After eight years of bloody war, Iran accepts the cease-fire with Iraq.

1989   Ayatollah Khomeini issues a religious edict for assassination of Salman Rushdie, the author of a book called *The Satanic Verses*.
Ayatollah Khomeini, the founder of Islamic Republic of Iran, dies.
Ayatollah Ali Khamenei becomes the new Supreme Leader.
Ali Akbar Rafsanjani becomes president.

1990   A major earthquake occurring in Manjil and Rudbar, the northern Iranian cities, kills about 50,000 people.
Iran and Iraq resume diplomatic relations after eight years of bloody wars that lasted from 1980 to 1988.

1995   United States imposes sanctions against Iran that include economic, trade, scientific, and military exchanges.

1997   Mohammad Khatami is elected by 70 percent of the vote as the new Iranian president due to his strong emphasis on civil society and government of law, political and social reform, and economic revitalization.

1999   Pro-democracy students' demonstrations after closure of a popular newspaper by the government turns bloody when government guards attack demonstrators.

2000   Pro-reform and supporters of Khatami win 189 of the 290 seats in the parliamentary elections, causing the liberals to control the legislature for the first time since the inception of the Islamic Republic in 1979.
In a continuous battle between the conservatives and liberals, the judiciary bans 16 reformist newspapers.

2001   Iran and Saudi Arabia sign a major security accord to combat terrorism, drug trafficking, and organized crime.
President Khatami is reelected for a second term with 77 percent of the vote.

2002   During his State of Union speech, U.S. president George W. Bush refers to Iraq, Iran, and North Korea as an "Axis of Evil."
Despite strong opposition from the U.S. government, the Russians begin construction of a major nuclear reactor in southern Iranian city of Bushehr.

2003	A military plane on its way from Zahedan to Kerman crashes on the Pakistani border, killing 302 passengers.
	Shirin Ebadi, a former judge and a human-rights activist, wins the Noble Peace Prize. Ebadi is the eleventh woman (and the first Muslim woman) to win such an award.
	The International Atomic Energy Agency (IAEA) announces that the Iranian government admits the production of plutonium, but emphasizes that there is no evidence that Iran is building nuclear weapons.
	On December 26, a major earthquake destroys the historic city of Bam in central Iran, killing about 30,000 and making more than 70,000 people homeless.
2004	After a controversial election, which was boycotted by many reformists, the conservatives reclaim control of the Iranian parliament.
2005	A major earthquake hits southern Iran, killing at least 500 people and injuring many more.
	Mahmoud Ahmadinejad, the former mayor of Tehran, who pledges ending economic corruption, forming egalitarian society, and returning to humane values of the 1979 revolution, wins the national election and becomes the new president.
2006	A military plane loaded with Iranian journalists crashes into a building in Tehran, killing about 115 passengers.
	Iranian president Ahmadinejad announces that Iran has successfully produced enough enriched uranium to make nuclear fuel.
	Iranian president Ahmadinejad sends a letter to U.S. president George W. Bush calling for mutual dialogue and ways to reduce tensions between the two governments.
2007	Iranian president Ahmadinejad visits the United States and gives a controversial talk at Columbia

145

University addressing U.S. and Israeli atrocities against Middle Eastern nations.

A new U.S. National Intelligence Estimate reports that Iran halted its nuclear weapon development program in 2003.

2008   Iran launches a rocket to inaugurate its newly built space research center. Conservatives win more than two-thirds of the seats in Iranian parliament when many reformist candidates are disqualified by the Guardian Council.

In an unprecedented move, President Ahmadinejad congratulates the newly elected U.S. president, Barack Obama.

Shirin Ebadi's human-rights center is raided and closed by the government.

2009   Iran announces country's launching of its first home-made satellite into space. State-run media announces Ahmadinejad as the winner of June 12 presidential election, but main opposition candidates allege vote-rigging; millions of Iranians demonstrate in streets of Tehran and other major Iranian cities, protesting the result. Clashes between government forces and demonstrators turn bloody and many are killed, and many others are arrested. Ahmadinejad is later pronounced the country's president for his second term.

UN Security Council members plus Germany propose an offer for Iran to enrich its uranium abroad, but Iran rejects the proposal and denounces it as "political." The Grand Ayatollah Hossein Ali Montazari, a leading figure of the 1979 Islamic Revolution and a vocal critic of the regime, dies at the age of 87.

2010   Iran makes a deal with Turkey and Brazil to send its uranium for enrichment, but Western states indicate that those deals do not stop uranium enrichment in Iran. UN Security Council votes in favor of imposing a new round of sanctions against Iran, which includes tighter finance curbs and expanded arms embargo.

Beeman, William O. *"The Great Satan" vs. "The Mad Mullahs."* Chicago: University of Chicago Press, 2008.

Gheissari, Ali, ed. *Contemporary Iran: Economy, Society, Politics.* New York: Oxford University Press, 2009.

Held, Colbert. *Middle East Patterns: Places, Peoples, and Politics.* 3rd edition. Boulder, Colo.: Westview Press, 2000.

Kheirabadi, Masoud. *Iranian Cities: Formation and Development.* Syracuse, N.Y.: Syracuse University Press, 2000.

———. *Islam.* New York: Chelsea House Publishers, 2004.

Milani, Mohsen. "Tehran's Take: Understanding Iran's U.S. Policy." *Foreign Affairs* (July/August 2009), pp. 45–62.

Pope, Arthur Upham. *A Survey of Persian Art.* London: Oxford University Press, 1938–1939.

Sadr, Hamid Reza. *Iranian Cinema: A Political History.* London: I.B. Tauris, 2006.

Sciolino, Elaine. *Persian Mirrors: The Elusive Face of Iran.* New York: Free Press, 2000.

Further Reading

Abrahamian, Ervand. *A History of Modern Iran.* New York: Cambridge University Press, 2008.

Ansari, Ali. *Confronting Iran: The Failure of American Foreign Policy and the Next Great Crisis in the Middle East.* New York: Basic Books, 2006.

Arberry, A.J. *The Legacy of Persia.* Oxford: Oxford University Press, 1953.

Arjomand, Said Amir. *The Turban for the Crown: The Islamic Revolution in Iran.* New York: Oxford University Press, 1988.

———. *After Khomeini: Iran Under His Successors.* New York: Oxford University Press, 2009.

Axworthy, Michael. *Empire of the Mind: A History of Iran.* New York: Basic Books, 2008.

Azimi, Fakhreddin. *The Quest for Democracy in Iran: A Century of Struggle Against Authoritarian Rule.* Cambridge, Mass.: Harvard University Press, 2008.

Buchta, Wilfried. *Who Rules Iran? The Structure of Power in the Islamic Republic.* Washington, D.C.: Washington Institute for Near East Policy, 2001.

Cottam, Richard. *Iran and the United States: A Cold War Case Study.* Pittsburgh: University of Pittsburgh Press, 1988.

Dabashi, Hamid. *Close Up: Iranian Cinema: Past, Present, and Future.* London: Verso Books, 2001.

Esposito, John. *Islam: The Straight Path.* New York: Oxford University Press, 1991.

Goode, James. *The United States and Iran: In the Shadow of Musaddiq.* New York: St. Martin's Press, 1997.

Hillmann, Michael. *Iranian Culture: A Persianist View.* Lanham, M.D.: University Press of America, 1990.

Karimi-Hakkak, Ahmad. *Recasting Persian Poetry: Scenarios of Poetic Modernity in Iran.* Salt Lake City: University of Utah Press, 1995.

Milani, Farzaneh. *Veils and Words.* Syracuse, N.Y.: Syracuse University Press, 1992.

O'Donnel, Terrence. *Garden of the Brave in War: Reflections of Iran.* Chicago: University of Chicago Press, 1980.

Osanloo, Arzoo. *The Politics of Women's Rights in Iran*. Princeton, N.J.: Princeton University Press, 2009.

Parsipur, Shahrnush. *Women Without Men*. Syracuse, N.Y.: Syracuse University Press, 1998.

Petrushevsky, I.P. *Islam in Iran*. Albany, N.Y.: State University of New York Press, 1985.

Sick, Gary. *All Fall Down: America's Tragic Encounter with Iran*. New York: Penguin Books, 1986.

Sullivan, Soraya. *Stories by Iranian Women Since the Revolution*. Austin, Tex.: University of Texas Press, 1990.

Wright, Robin. *The Last Great Revolution: Turmoil and Transformation in Iran*. New York: Vintage Books, 2001.

Web Sites

Amnesty International
http://www.amnesty.org

CIA World Factbook
https://www.cia.gov/library/publications/the-world-factbook

International Monetary Fund
http://www.imf.org/external

Islamic Republic of Iran
http://www.mideastinfo.com/iran.htm

The National Iranian American Council
http://cyberiran.com/history

Statistical Center of Iran
http://www.unescap.org/pop/popin/profiles/iran/popin2.htm

Statistical, Economic and Social Research and Training Center for Islamic Countries
http://www.sesrtcic.org/defaulteng.shtml

U.S. Energy Information Administration
http://www.eia.doe.gov/cabs/Iran/Oil.html

Picture Credits

Index

Index

Index

MASOUD KHEIRABADI is an Iranian American who immigrated to the United States in 1976. He lived three years in Texas, where he received his M.S. in agricultural mechanization from Texas A&I University (which later joined with Texas A&M). In 1979, he moved to Eugene, Oregon, and studied at the University of Oregon, where he received his M.A. and later Ph.D. in geography. He has taught at the University of Oregon, Lewis and Clark College, and Maryhurst University. He is currently teaching for the International Studies Program at Portland State University.

Kheirabadi's research interest focuses on issues and problems of development in less-developed countries, with a regional emphasis on the Middle East. He is interested in issues concerning resource management, sustainable development, urbanization, population, race and ethnic relations, and cultural geography. Dr. Kheirabadi has published several books and articles on Middle Eastern issues. His books include *Iranian Cities: Formation and Development, Islam* (WORLD GREAT RELIGIONS), and *Sri Satya Sai Baba* (SPIRITUAL LEADERS AND THINKERS.)

CHARLES F. "FRITZ" GRITZNER is Distinguished Professor Emeritus of Geography at South Dakota State University in Brookings. In 2010, he retired from teaching after a 50-year career, during which he taught more than 70 different courses. In retirement, Fritz, his wife, Yvonne, and their "family" of two Italian greyhounds will remain in South Dakota. He enjoys traveling, writing, and sharing his love for and knowledge of geography with readers. As a senior consulting editor and frequent author for Chelsea House Publishers (MODERN WORLD NATIONS, MAJOR WORLD CULTURES, EXTREME ENVIRONMENTS, and GLOBAL CONNECTIONS series), Fritz has a wonderful opportunity to combine each of these "hobbies." Dr. Gritzner has served as both president and executive director of the National Council for Geographic Education (NCGE) and has received the council's highest honor, the George J. Miller Award for Distinguished Service to Geographic Education, as well as numerous other national teaching, service, and research recognitions from the NCGE, the Association of American Geographers, and other organizations.